SOCIAL CHANGE IN MANIPUR

SOCIAL CHANGE IN MANIPUR

Editor

B.K. Ahluwalia

Shashi Ahluwalia

GYAN

Published by

Gyan Publishing House
5, Ansari Road
Daryaganj, New Delhi-110002
Phone: 011-47034999, 9811692060
E-mail: books@gyanbooks.com

Distribution Network
gyanbooks.com
India, USA, Canada, UK, Australia, France

ISBN: 978-81-212-2353-9 (HB)

First Published, 1984

Printed at: Gyan Press, Delhi.

SOCIAL CHANGE IN MANIPUR
Editor: B.K. Ahluwalia, Shashi Ahluwalia

List of Illustrations

Between pages 32 and 33

1. Shri Jawaharlal Nehru giving away prizes to Manipur Contingent
2. Prime Minister Smt. Indira Gandhi with folk dancers
3. Smt. Indira Gandhi being garlanded on her arrival at Imphal
4. Smt. Indira Gandhi addressing in Imphal
5. Polo game being played in Imphal
6. Wrestling in Manipuri style
7. Folk dancers of Manipur in Delhi
8. Raslila of Manipur
9. Manipuri couple singing a bhajan
10. Folk dancers at Rajpath in New Delhi on Republic Day
11. Smt. Indira Gandhi with Manipuri women at Raj Bhavan, Imphal
12. Indian National Army Stupa in Imphal
13. Folk dancers of Manipur
14. A Manipuri girl in a bridal dress
15. Statue of Netaji at the Indian National Army Martyrs Memorial Ground unveiled by Shri V.V. Giri, then President of India
16. Shri V.V. Giri inaugurates the Martyrs Memorial Stupa.

Between pages 80 and 81

17. Manipur Tableaux moving down Rajpath, New Delhi during Republic Day Parade
18. The Chairman, Trade Fair Authority of India, presenting the First Award to the representative of Manipur Pavilion in 1981

Preface

MANIPUR has been described by many as the 'Jewel of India'. And rightly too. Nestling amid hills which stand towering in the North East of India and overlooking the rugged terrain of Burma, Manipur occupies a distinct place in the geo-political map of India.

Nature has been profusely bounteous to Manipur. The hills and the dales and the thick vegetation keep it verdant green all the year round making it a tourist's delight.

The State is rich in tradition and history. The influence of the Krishna cult, with its stress on gaiety and cheer, breathes into the land all that is exclusive to its character. The dance and the music of the land spring from their intrinsic trait of the tolerant Hinduism.

In consonance with the natural setting, the people are rustic, simple and largely untouched by the pollution of modern living. Their wants are few, they love outdoor life, find communion with nature and depend on the gifts of nature like rice for food, fish to supplement their dish.

The book captures the subtle nuances of the State, brings through crisp narrative a clear picture of the State, its culture and its people. The traditions and the customs of the people are detailed with such skill that the reader finds himself transported there. The authors recreate the scenic beauty of the State with its hills, valleys and rivulets, through words and also through illustrations.

Manipur is marching towards economic prosperity and has already reached the threshold of overall development. With economic development, changes are also bound to take place in social and cultural fields. The work also depicts the socio-eco-cultural transformation of the State in the recent years.

The authors are grateful to the contributors for their articles and also to the Publications Division, Government of India, *Marg* and *Indian Literature* for permission to reproduce material from their publications. They are also indebted to the Librarians and staff of Nehru Memorial Museum Library and Research & Reference Division Library for their valuable help.

The authors are also grateful to Prof. K. Swaminathan and S/Shri V. Narayanswamy, J.P. Uniyal and R.K. Murthi who had been kind enough to give many useful suggestions.

B-13/505, Lodi Colony,
New Delhi-110003
29th February, 1984

B.K. AHLUWALIA
SHASHI AHLUWALIA

Contents

1. The Land of Jewels 1
—*B.K. Ahluwalia*

2. Manipuri Dance 24
—*Kapila Vatsyayan*

3. Martial Arts 37
—*E. Nilakanta Singh*

4. Manipuri Language 46
—*N. Tombi Singh*

5. Literature 52
—*Jyotirmoy Roy*

6. Culture 60
—*R.K. Jhalajit Singh*

7. Daring Dames of Manipur 72
—*R.K. Murthi*

8. Towards Prosperity 79
—*Shashi Ahluwalia*

APPENDICES

I. Origin of the Manipuris 111

II. Religion of Manipuris 136

To
Meenakshi, Shobhana and Rajesh

1

The Land of Jewels

B. K. Ahluwalia

MANIPUR literally means the "Land of gems" and has been referred to by the various connotations like "Jewel of India", "a little paradise", "a flower on lofty heights", and "the Kashmir of Eastern India". In the olden days it had been called by a variety of names. The Burmese called it *Ka-the* and *Ka-se*, and the Assamese *Mekheli* and *Mogalou.* To the people of Cachar in Assam it was *Mogli.*

There are a number of versions as to how the State came to be known as Manipur. According to some it came to be known as such because there was much diamond ore in the area in ancient times, 'Mani' meaning diamond and 'pur' meaning place, there are others who aver that Manipur means "beautiful garden".

The legend goes that when the country was at one time waterlogged, Lord Shiva and Uma, who in Manipur are known as Nagpokningthon and Panthoibi respectively descended upon it and performed the Lai Haraoba dance. The entire country was lit up day and night by the snake god Ananta, who came to see the dance with the magic gem (Mani) on his hood. From this, Manipur got the name 'The City of Gem'.

It had been described as the "Switzerland of India" by Lord Irwin. It is so like Switzerland that the beauty of the surroundings, the softness of the air and the richness of the pastures are soothing to the tourists. Its exotic scenery and mystic atmosphere are Nature's masterpiece to match with Switzerland.

Manipur is a small hilly State in the North-Eastern Region. Its total area is 22,356 sq. km. with 1813 sq. km. of fertile valley in its centre. Manipur is bounded by Nagaland in the north, Mizoram in the south, Burma in the east and Cachar District of Assam in the west. Its population is 14.5 lakhs (1981 census). Out of them more thàn two thirds are plains people while the 29 tribes such as Nagas, Kukis and other tribes take their abode in the hills. Imphal, the capital city, is located in the valley.

It has a healthy and salubrious climatic conditions. The evergreen scenic beauty and large fields dotted with shining lakes are indeed enchanting.

Manipur came under the British Rule in 1891. It was merged with the Indian Union in October, 1949. The Advisory form of Government introduced in 1950-51 was replaced by a Territorial Council providing 30 elected and two nominated members. Manipur became a full-fledged State of India on the 21st January, 1972. Our Prime Minister, Smt. Indira Gandhi, inaugurated this twentieth State of our Union. The occasion marked the fulfilment of the long cherished desire of the people of Manipur.

Out of the 60 Assembly Constituencies, 19 seats are reserved for the Scheduled Tribes. Manipur is represented in the Lok Sabha by two Members (one is reserved for the Scheduled Tribes) and in the Rajya Sabha by one Member (General).

The plains people are mostly Meiteis (Hindus) and Muslims. The link language is Manipuri which has been adopted as State Official Language since early 1980.

The Meities of Manipur claim to be descendants of an Indo-Chinese stock with an admixture of Aryan blood. They dominate the valley district of Imphal with a population of nearly 10 lakhs. When the Aryan race was still in its progressive and colonizing stage, Manipur was repeatedly invaded. In the process, many settled down in Manipur and married Manipuri girls. The *Manipur Puran* traces the royal lineage of the kings of the State to Babhruvahana, the son of Arjuna, the third hero of Mahabharata who came to Manipur and married Chitrangada, daughter of the then Gandharva King Chitrasen of Manipur. However, according to some scholars, Manipur mentioned in Mahabharata is in Orissa. But people of Manipur claim that Manipur of Mahabharata is identical with the present state of Manipur.

The influx of Brahmins from other parts of the country during the last 500 years had added yet more to the admixture of bloods. They married Meiti girls and settled in Manipur itself.

Around 1250 AD, a large Chinese force attacked Manipur but the attack was repulsed and the Chinese suffered heavy losses. Of the prisoners who survived, many settled down in Manipur and their descendants are still to be seen among the Manipuris.

In 1819, when Burmese had invaded Manipur in large strength, the Manipuris fled into Assam beyond Cachar.

In 1825, with the help of Mr. David Scott, the British agent to the Governor General, a young Manipuri prince raised a force known as Manipur Levy and attacked the Burmese and drove them out of Manipur into Burma beyond the Kabow valley.

The dress of the Manipuris is very colourful.

The men folks normally wear trousers and shirts but the older folks wear the traditional white *dhoti* and *kurta* A small cloth piece with check prints is normally carried on the shoulders to serve as hand-towel. The women folks wear the normal blouse and a cloth known as "Phanek" and drape it across the shoulder as a saree. This dress is akin to the dress worn by teenaged girls in the southern parts of our country.

Women from well-to-do families wear necklace, chain and other ornaments as worn by women in other parts of our country. The men folks and even children wear gold chains.

Though due to the influence of economic development and impact of Western culture most of the customs and traditions are on the wane among Manipuris yet it would be of interest to know about some of their customs.

When a marriage is to be arranged, the boy along with a companion has to go to the girl's house. They would be seated on a mat known as "Kouna-phak". The girl would then place a "sarei" (smoking pipe made of banana leaf) and a "nagthaks" (pot with sweet smelling tobacco) for the young guests. The boy would understand the approval or disapproval of the girl from the length of the pipe. A long pipe indicated rejection and a short pipe indicated acceptance of the boy by the girl.

Feasts form an important part of Manipuri culture. In any social feast the cook must be a Brahmin. In the feasts hosted by rich men, the number of dishes must be 108. Even in a feast hosted by an average Manipuri family a large number of dishes are generally served. Fish is served only in non-religious feasts. Manipuris do not usually eat meat.

Manipuris are crazy about fish and they breed fish in their household tanks known as "Pukhri". Fish is sold in the market at a very high price.

Marriages mostly take place between the months of October and April. During and after Holi, the youths take part in a traditional Manipuri folk dance known as "Thabal Chongba". In the course of this dance which is held daily over a period of five to eight days the males and the females select their life-partners and later elope. On their return to the village after a few days, their marriage is solemnised. Though "Thabal Chongba" is still held with much fanfare and enthusiasm, the tradition of choosing the marriage partners is gradually on the wane. These days young boys and girls take part in this dance just to keep up the tradition.

In Manipur when a person dies the dead body is placed in the south east corner of the courtyard, where a small thatch hut called 'Khangpok' without the side walls is erected for the purpose. Instead of the side wall, a white cloth is put all around, so that the dead body is not clearly visible. All the friends and relatives of the deceased pay their homage in this hut.

The funeral takes place at the bank of a river. Before placing the body on the pyre, it is bathed in the river. Such a bath is believed to sanctify the dead body.

In the Manipuri society, Maibis, the local physicians who cure various ailments by giving herbal medicines, hold important positions. Even the mid-wives who attend to maternity cases are known as Maibis. Some Maibis are known to possess certain supernatural powers as that of dealing with evil spirits.

Manipuris are very religious people. Even their music and dances are based on religious themes. Hardly any aspect of their life can be dissociated from their deep love for religion.

It is a common sight to see a basil plant (Tulsi) grown in front of the house of any Manipuri. In the north eastern corner of the courtyard a small temple is usually built where all food preparations are offered to the deity.

Today the lifestyle of Manipuris is distinct from that of the people of other States of the country but the influence of Western culture is on the increase and Manipuris are giving up their age-old traditions.

The flora of Manipur is rich in the variety. It is due to diversity in temperature and rainfall in different parts of the State. A part of Manipur i.e. Jirighat is only 39.3 metres above the sea-level whereas another part is well above 2,700 metres. So the vegetation of the plains differs from that of the mountains.

Most of the flora of Manipur is similar to that of Assam, Bhutan and Upper Burma. Manipur is rich in aquatic flowers like the lotus and water-lily. The gorgon fruit (*Eurale fero*) called *thangjing* in Manipuri and *makhana* in Hindi and a small variety of water-chestnut (Hindi *singara*, Manipuri *heikak*) grow here. Manipur has an abundant variety of beautiful orchids.

In the valley, one can still see *Carthamus tinctorious* (Sanskrit *kusumbha*, Manipuri *kusum lei*) once carefully cultivated as a dye-crop for its beautiful colour in Spain, southern Germany, Italy, Hungary, southern Russia and Bangladesh.

Manipur has a rich variety of fauna. In Manipur we find the goral (Manipuri *Sabeng*) which is essentially an animal of cold regions. There is also the *Hyelaphus porcinus* (Manipuri *Kharsha*), an animal of the hot south-east Asia. Many animals and birds are those that are common in eastern India. Tiger, leopard, bear and wolf are found in hill forests. Sambur, spotted deer and barking deer were commonly found here many years ago. The Manipuri deer (*Cervus eldi*) has become rare. Some species of the monkey are also found.

Manipur is best introduced through her dances. The well-known festival of Lai Haraoba, mostly performed between the spring and the rainy season, is the most comprehensive feast of dances. The term "Lai Haraoba" means the festivity of gods and goddesses. The Raasa Lila, one of the classical dances of India enacting Shri Krishna's love of Radha and Gopis, is marvellous and has tremendous value with its devotional theme. The costumes are unique and colourful. The different 29 hill tribes inhabiting the rugged areas of the State are also proud of their rich culture. Their rich culture is reflected in their cloth designs and other works of art. Their folk-dances are colourful and enchant the onlookers.

The different varieties of Manipur dances are :

1. Lai Haraoba Dance
2. Krishna Vandana
3. Sword Fighting
4. Mao-Maram Naga Dance
5. Pena-Music
6. Kabui Naga Dance
7. Nata Sankirtana
8. Basanta Raas

1. *Lai Haraoba Dance* : Lai Haraoba, merry-making with the gods, is the traditional festival of great importance to

the people of Manipur. Through this festival the people of Manipur have been keeping the concept of their origin and mode of life through the centuries. The Maibas and Maibis conduct the entire ceremony in which the creation of the world, the birth of life and growth of civilization etc., are enacted through complicated rituals. This dance is performed all over Manipur in front of particular deities. Girls and boys of the area also participate in this dance.

2. *Krishna-Vandana* : This dance represents an invocation to Lord Krishna. The dancer performs *Abhinaya* on song from "Geet Govinda" of poet Jaya Dev beginning with "Shrita Kamala Kucha". The song describes various attributes of Lord Krishna.

3. *Sword Fighting* : Martial arts were one of the most important and compulsory subjects of Manipuri boys and girls irrespective of age in the ancient days for self-defence etc. In this fight the two sword fighters demonstrate their skill and ability to attack upon the enemy and defend themselves.

4. *Mao-Maram Naga Dance* : This is the most important merry-making dance of Mao-Maram Naga people inhabiting a hill village in the Manipur North District about 106 km. from Imphal. It is performed during the great annual festival lasting about 15 days. During this festival friends and dear ones are invited for community feast and dancing.

5. *Pena Music* : Pena is an indigenous stringed instrument of Manipur associated with the ballad-singing. This ancient instrument accompanies the "Lai Haraoba" festival. Playing on the Pena, the musician sings an episode from the immortal epic of Manipur "Khamba-Thoibi". The song describes how Khamba, the hero of the story, subdued a wild bull.

6. *Kit-Lam* (Kabui Naga Dance) : This is one of the most popular dances of Kabui tribe of Manipur. It is known for its vigorous footwork and graceful movement of the body. This particular dance depicts the dance of legendary cricket performed in a competition before the Kabui god.

7. *Nata-Sankirtana* : This particular presentation is only

a piece but a dominant feature of Manipuri Nata Sankirtana. The dancers sing in praise of Shri Gouranga while executing rhythmic and vigorous movements to the combined sound of the Kartal and Pung (Mridanga).

8. *Basanta Raas* : This is a sequence from the Basanta Raas of Manipur played in the fullmoon night of Chaitra (March-April). Krishna went to the appointed grove for his Divine sports with the Gopis. The Gopis led by Radha responded to the call of his flute and met him and they danced together tbrowing *Abeer*, the red powder, at each other. The end comes with "Milan", the union of Lord Krishna with Radha.

Manipur is the birth place of the game of Polo. Here men even above 80 years of age play this game with great zeal and enthusiasm. Other Manipuri traditional games like Mukna-kangjei (Manipuri freestyle hockey cum wrestling) and Yudi Lanpi (snatching of coconut) are fascinating and enchant onlookers. Manipuri players and athletes are now in the national records.

There are many legends and myths about the origin of the different varieties of handloom products of Manipur. All these point to the fact that the handloom industry in Manipur developed gradually with the emergence of an organised society in this small State. Handloom industry is the back-bone of Manipur's economy and it continues to be a major source of income of the people. The interesting thing one notices in the handloom industry is the amalgamation of the aesthetic aspirations and sense of the people with a consumable material product in the form of beautiful sarees, ningthouphee, lelrum, lashingphee, mayek naiba etc. are names of different items of handloom product.

Manipuri women through the ages produced wonderful varieties of cloth weaving on the loin looms and the Pangyong (throw shuttle). The products of these unsophisticated looms are simply wonderful in texture, finish and durability. Manipuri women are famous weavers and the knowledge of weaving is an essential qualification of a woman in the Manipuri society.

Manipuri handloom is respected to be one of the oldest industries in the country. However it had been modernised around 1921 when two local entrepreneurs S/Shri K. Tombi Singh and H. Keipha Singh manufactured fly shuttle loom to weave cloth.

Around 1924, Mrs. Jolly, Private Tutoress to Her Highness Maharani Dhanamanjuri Devi of Manipur, engaged some expert Manipuri female weavers to produce fabrics of European taste with combination of Manipuri designs at her residence. Her venture was obstructed because the weavers were new in the line and she herself was not well conversant with Manipuri language through which she had to communicate with the weavers.

Later, Mrs. Jolly obtained the services of the two local entrepreneures who got training in handloom weaving from a textile institute outside the State. With their help and cooperation, she could establish an Institute of Arts and Crafts of Manipur which was sanctioned by the then President of Manipur State Darbar, Captain Harvey. Mrs. Jolly was the first manager of the Institute. Later, when Mrs. Jolly left the State for good, His Highness, the Maharaja of Manipur, Sir Churachand Singh, appointed Shri K. Tombi Singh as the second manager of the Institute in 1936 in recognition of his sagacity, ingenuity, ability for innovation and phenomenal success in bringing about a total change in the handloom industry of Manipur. The Institute made good progress but collapsed in 1942 as it was hit by bombs during World War II in which Imphal suffered a lot. Again in 1948, an Arts and Weaving House was established at the initiative of Shri Tombi Singh. This organisation has been a major firm in the line of production of standardised handloom fabrics with composition of various original designs of the hills and the valley of Manipur in modernised forms to cater to different tastes and requirements of all classes of people in India and abroad.

In the modern age, the Industries Department under the Government of Manipur in collaboration with local weaving experts has been making all efforts to promote Manipur handloom and handicrafts. It has opened a number of Handloom Production Centres, Design Centres, Training Centres, etc. As part of the Manipur Government's Handloom and Handicrafts development scheme, Manipur Handloom and Handicrafts Development Corporation has been set up with a view to further promote its handloom and handicraft products. The Manipur Handloom and Handicrafts Emporia at Calcutta and Delhi are also playing vital role in promoting the sales and gaining popularity by taking part in national and International handloom and handicrafts exhibitions held in important centres of the country from time to time.

Of the numerous colourful handicrafts of Manipur special mention may be made of their textiles with tribal designs in vigorous colours, traditional dolls of straw and clay, jewellery, strong bell metal bowls, cane and bamboo, and mats made with spongy reeds. Almost every house in Manipur has a loom. Handloom products and quilts (lashingphee) of Manipur are in great demand at home and abroad. In this age of synthetic fibre, Manipuri women still continue to use handloom *chadar* and it forms part of their ceremonial dress. The tribal people produce fine textiles. The Naga shawl has all India repute. The Handloom and Handicrafts Development Corporation in Manipur, a state government undertaking, has not spared any effort to promote economic conditions of the weavers especially to boost up the sale of Manipuri handloom and handicrafts by opening various emporia at different places in the country.

According to D. N. Saroj, "Tribal textiles are woven on a loin loom, a type of back strap loom commonly used by hill people. The warp of manageable length and breadth is prepared and fastened at one end, generally to the wall of a house or two fixed poles, while the other is tied to the waist of the weaver with a cotton or leather belt. Sometimes the belt is woven out of cane or bamboo.

"Handloom weaving is the most important craft of the State. Every girl knows how to weave and is given a loom as part of her dowry. It is estimated that handloom products worth Rs. 75 lakhs are produced annually, of which 30 per cent go outside the State. In Imphal town and the neighbouring villages weaving is mostly done on fly-shuttle looms. The "Lasingphee" (quilted cotton material) produced in Manipur and used as a covering in winter would do well in a new range of designs.

"The tribals in the State, who number slightly more than 1,00,000, are all agriculturists. Weaving is a common craft practised by almost every housewife. The Tang Khuls, Kukis and Kabuis are known for their artistically woven shawls and wrappers. The finewarp striped *phaneks* woven on loin looms in the valley are beautiful examples of traditional craft. Vegetable dyes are still used for part of the dyeing ; for instance, the juice of the wild indigo is used to obtain a black or dark dark blue dye, while green and yellow are produced from the bark of jungle trees.

"The areas around Imphal have a tradition of weaving which reveals the influence of a sophisticated culture." Morangfi sarees woven in white or soft colours carry a *mandir shikhara* temple top) on the border with dotted patterns on the body. There is a belief that this pattern was created by the goddess Morangfi herself. The *idkli*, though called a bottle design, is actually a copy of a loom accessory. It is very popular and widely used on shoulder bags and bedcovers with flowered designs. Then there are figured designs on borders resembling jamdani, with horses, swords and spears for use in rituals. *Shamilami* is a combination of weaving and embroidery, once considered a status symbol. The *maibung* is said to be a copy of a natural design, resembling the grains of wood as revealed when it is chopped clean. *Hijamayak*, which is a boat form, has a restricted use as it is associated with death ceremonies. People wear a variety of shawls, and have adopted a number of patterns from tribal designs for weaving bedcovers, stoles and table cloths.

Manipur has only one style of embroidery with practically no variety in stitches. "This embroidery is done on the border of tbe *phanek*, a multicoloured piece of cloth worn by Manipuri women in a dark matching shade with untwisted silk thread, the colour usually being dark red, plum or chocolate. It is so finely made and evenly formed that it seems to be part of the weave and is often taken as such. The *phanek* is sometimes a plain fabric in a dark shade or with plain stripes in three colours, so that this embroidery is the only adornment it has. But in its restraint lies its charm and dignity.

"The most significant design in Manipuri embroidery is the *akoybi*. The colours used in the design are two shades of red with a little black and just a touch of white. Among other emboidered designs, mention may be made of the animal motifs seen on the black shawls which are called Angami Naga shawls."

Manipur is also famous for its beautiful baskets. Intricate patterns with dyed bamboo are worked on these baskets. A special feature of Manipuri basketware is the variety of bamboo fish traps which are so exquisitely crafted as to be almost sculptural. Another variety of baskets, the *chengbon*, have a domed lid made of bamboo. These have a square body of checks and squares in black and white, and rest on four prominent legs, and are used for storing clothes. Excellent reed mats and cushions are also woven in Manipur. Known locally as *kounaphak* they are made in the sizes, 22"×30" and 18"+18" respectively. Another type of double-weave mat known as *phak* is also woven in the State. These, as well as the mats and baskets, are in great demand outside Manipur.

Bell metal, locally known as *senjeng*, is an important metal, not only for the manufacture of household utensils but for other objects of art as well. One particular item, the *Sengabetel* container is specially popular. Among other important items mention may be made of the Krishna Kanti dish in the shape of a large bowl, with a broad encircling rim at the neck, resting on a small pedestal. Old references date the bell metal craft of Manipur to the late 17th or early 18th century. It is still a cottage industry and is virtually confined to two areas of the valley, viz. Heirangkhoithong (at Chinga Makha) and Aheibam Leikai (at Khongnang Pheidekpi). Both are about four miles south of Imphal and are three miles apart. There are about 300 households engaged in this craft, all expert in the moulding and casting brass, copper, bronze and bell metal. The craftsmen in the two villages produce plain metal bowls as well those with surface decoration, which are in great demand. One craftsman was the recipient of the National Award (1977) for his outstanding work.

The products of the Manipur bell metal industry derive much of their aesthetic vitality from the ancient art. The possibility of exploring foreign markets for these products has not yet been fully studied.

Manipur is also famous for beautiful dolls and toys of straw and clay. The most popular among them are representations of Lord Krishna, local deities and dancing figures. These dolls are delicately modelled and decorated.

Manipur is also known for its gold and gold-plated jewellery. Beautifully designed old jewellery displayed in the State Museum is being reproduced in silver.

A big project to develop tasar silk is under way in Manipur. With the weaving skill available in this area, a variety of tasar fabrics could be woven in quantity, as expansion of tasar yarn production takes place. The Weavers Service Centre of the All India Handloom Board, located at Imphal, has already done commendable experimental work in this direction.

Sericulture is being patronised by Manipur. Manipur is a land of oaks of many species gifted by nature. The natural tall trees are made dwarf bushes by cutting from time to time for fuel. Manipur Tasar is based on these dwarf bushes of oaks. The main oaks used in Tasar culture are: Uyung, Sahi and Chakpa Uyung. It is estimated that oaks cover two lakh acres.

Antherea proylei-oak tasar silk worm reared for tasar cocoons is a hybrid of A. pernii (Chinese race) and A. roylei

(Indian race). This bybrid is a very promising one. This hybrid is teramoulter with five insters during the larval period. This hybrid silk worm spins cocoons with the formation of peduncle. The quality of cocoon is far better than both parent races. The silk worms feed on oak leaves of the shrubs in the open field for about a month. Spin cocoons are the raw material for tasar silk.

Conversion of cocoons into silk yarn is the next step. Reeling and spinning are the main devices for extraction of silk from cocoons. Silk yarn produced through Reeling Process is known as reeled yarn and spun yarn out of spinning. The size of reeled yarn may be made according to the requirement from superfine to fine. The common type of tasar yarn are—Reeled yarn, Gheecha, Charkha Spun and Jhuri (hand-drawn out of silk wastes). The tasar silk yarns of this hybrid race are reported to be of very good quality comparable to those of China.

The tasar yarns are raw material for traditional exquisite handloom industry of Manipur and of other States of India, mostly for exports. As Manipur is having her own rich traditional designs of handloom industry the silk yarns produced from tasar cocoons are utilised for weaving of silk fabrics of different varieties and designs. Suitings, shirtings, sarees, chaddars are the main tasar silk products of handloom.

Manipur Tasar is free from artificiality and admixtures. It is natural reeled or spun silk. Unlike a synthetic or mixed product, Manipur Tasar gives you the real soft and silken feel—the natural tenderness, cool and warmth of a loving and caring mother. Instead of spoilage and fading of colour, its beauty and utility grow with the years that pass. With every wash it brightens up and gains a new and more elegant look, which is why people like to wear and use Manipur Tasar.

The Manipuris have a number of religious festivals. Lai Haraoba is one such important festival in which the ancient deities of Pre-Hinduism days are worshipped. It needs mention here that Hinduism engulfed the Manipur valley of Imphal only about 300 years ago, while the adjoining hill district remained un-influenced. In the dance-drama performed on the occasion of Lai Haraoba, the Maibis are known to play leading roles. The creation of life and growth of civilization is depicted in the dance-drama which extends over a period of 10 to 15 days. This is generally followed by holding of sports meet in which young men and women take active part.

Cheiraoba is another important festival. People clean and decorate their houses and enjoy sumptuous food after a part of it has been offered to various deities. It is celebrated on the first day of the year. The villagers rush to the nearest hill tops under the belief that such climb to lofty heights will enable them to rise to greater heights in worldly life.

It may be mentioned that all devotional songs and prayers are in Bengali language than in Manipuri. Prayers and songs in the local Meitei language are strictly forbidden in the Royal Shri Govindji temple. In the late Twenties of this century there was a revolt by school students pressing for the use of Manipuri language in the singing of devotional songs. After the revolt Manipuri language is used in the singing of songs during Holi festival. Although the modern youths are pressing the use of Manipuri language in all religious functions, the elders do not approve of this. But it may not be long before Manipuri gets to be used as the sole language of devotional ceremonies.

Dol-Yatra (Yaosang) festival is a five-day festival in March dedicated to Lord Gouranga according to Vaisnavism. During the festival, Manipur is agog with sound of dance music "Thabal Chongba", which is associated with this festival. This is the Manipuri term of Holi and is considered to be the biggest festival in Manipur for the Hindus.

The second biggest festival of the Hindus in Manipur is the Ratha-Yatra or Car Festival lasting eight days in June/July. Lord Jagannath leaves his temple in a car pulled by mass of pilgrims who vie with one another for this honour. The goddess Durga is propitiated during Durga Puja, held in October. Goddess Lakshmi is welcomed by all house-holds during Diwali in October/November with small oil lamps. Besides these, the Krishna Janmashtami, Radhaashtmi, Heikru

Hidongba, Ningol Chak Kouba etc. are also important festivals of the Manipuri Hindus. Manipuri Hindus celebrate New Year's Day in the second week of April with traditional and conventional programmes.

Imphal (over 780 meters above M.S.L.) is the capital of Manipur. Its area is 1813 sq. km. Imphal is generally divided into two parts namely the Municipality area and its periphery known as the Greater Imphal. Its population is around two lakhs 60% of which is in the Municipal area. According to the legends of Manipur the entire Manipur valley was submerged under water for thousands of years. The water was drained out towards the Burma valley by cutting a tunnel through the hill ranges on the Indo-Burma border. The idea and execution of the tunnel is attributed to supernatural being known by different names. The accurate time of the tunnelling has now gone into oblivion or to put it more precisely, into the unwritten pages of the legends of the land. The belief in the episode of the extraordinary tunnel is known as Chingnung Hut in Manipuri. Those who have seen it acclaim that it looks miraculous. The waterfall gushing out of it is said to be so powerful that people can pass under the water roof without drenching themselves. Scholars believe that the Imphal portion of the valley dried up first facilitating the earliest settlements in it.

Imphal was the capital of one of the seven principalities thriving in keen competition in Manipur. Its importance was greatly enhanced after the unification of Manipur as one kingdom under a single ruler who had Imphal as his capital. The unification process started from the time of King Garivniwaz and was completed during the reign of Rajarishi Bhagyachandra. When the East India Company started having links with Manipur in the 18th century Manipur was an integrated kingdom.

Today it has more than 35 secondary schools, 15 degree colleges and a university. The colleges include a Regional Medical College, an agricultural college, a music college and an art college. The Jawaharlal Nehru Manipur Dance Academy sponsored by the Sangeet Natak Akademi deserves a special mention. The Industrial Training Institute and the Government Polytechnic are, among others, the main centres for technical training.

Two rivers, namely, the Imphal and Nambul rivers pass through the heart of Imphal city. Small rivulets like the Kongba and the Naga also touch Imphal. The capital city is surrounded by beautiful hills. Standing anywhere in the heart of the city one can see the dignified Nongmaijing hills in the east and the Langol in the north. The western hill ranges are not far from the city. The greater part of Imphal grew up unplanned. A tourist will be surprised to see the city-dwellers still retaining their earlier mode of living in self-sufficient premises which invariably contain a small tank, a bamboo grove, a kitchen garden, outdoor sanitary system, one or two outhouses and spacious courtyard flanked by the outhouses and the main dwelling house. Times are, however, changing fast, lifestyle too is following suit. What one sees today in the town may not be seen after a decade. An aerial view of the city gives a unique sight.

The Khwairamband is the main market of the State. Its southern wing is named after Poona Branabashi, the hero of Kongiom war of 1891. Northern wing after General Thangal who was hanged along with Bir Tikendrajit Singh soon after the British conqest of Manipur in August, 1891. The road running from the heart of the bazar to the western gate of the old palace, now used by the 4th Bn. Assam Rifles, has been named after Tikendrajit. The highlight of the bazar is its vendor-stalls run by women only. The commodities sold by the women vendors, their number running into thousands, are handloom products, vegetables, fish and fruits, etc. The other smaller markets are Singjamei, Kongba, Iamlong, Kwakethel, Heirangoithong, Tera Keithel, Naoremthong Keisam-thong, etc.

In close neighbourhood of the Khwai Bazar, the Pologround famous for its polo games during the British days provide facilities for all modern games and sports. Polo has been shifted from it. Adjoining the Pologround, the Bir Tikendrajit

Park, now decorated by a tall Minar commemorating patriots, gives added attraction to the sacred spot now used for public meetings and rallies. Next stands the oldest high school, the Johnstone Higher Secondary School, which was established at the end of the last century before the British conquest.

There are some regular theatre houses of which the Manipur Dramatic Union, the Rupmahal Theatre and the Aryan Theatre deserve special mention.

The area now occupied by the 4th Bn. Assam Rifles was the old palace of the independent rulers of Manipur. It contains many valuable historical and archeological monuments. The present Govindjee Temple with two golden domes and the massive congregation hall (an iron structure) were built after the British conquest.

The Hanuman Mandir inside a beautiful grove on the bank of the Imphal river and near the new palace compound is one of the oldest Hindu temples. It was constructed in the early part of the seventeenth century. The Ramji Prabhu Mandir and the big tank near it, the biggest of its kind in the State, has tremendous historical and cultural importance. The old Kangla moat surrounding the old palace has now been renovated as Kangla Park to provide special attraction to the city.

Two War Cemeteries, one for the Christians and the other for the Indian Armies particularly for those heroes who were killed in the Second World War maintained by the Commonwealth War Graves Commission, are remarkable for their symmetry and serenity. Those who love peace or solace should visit the War Cemeteries situated on the Imphal-Dimapur National Highway and another on the Imphal-Ukhrul road about 1.5 km. from the heart of the city.

The State Museum near the Imphal Pologround provides a panorama of Manipur including tribal culture and on display are wide varieties of costumes, arms of war and peace, historical documents, relics, etc. It is growing as a full-fledged museum attracting large number of visitors.

The climate of Manipur is salubrious. The cold weather

lasts from October to February. Winter in some hill areas is severe. Rain falls from April to October.

Manipur is connected with road and rail. Dimapur, 215 km. from Imphal is the nearest Railway Station. The National Highway No. 39 leading to Dimapur in Nagaland passes through the State of Nagaland connecting Manipur with the rest of India. The other 225 km. long National Highway No. 53 Imphal-Jiribam Road connecting Silchar District in Assam is the second lifeline of Manipur. It links Imphal with the rest of the country via Silchar where there is a Railway Station.

The following are tbe places worth seeing in Manipur.

About seven km. off Imphal there is the Zoological Garden at Iroishemba on the Imphal-Kangchup Road. It is popularly known as Mini Zoo and is famous for its inmate Brow antlered Deer, the rarest species which are found only in Manipur. A trip to this garden at the foot of the pine growing hillocks and in the westernmost corner of Lamphelpat is enjoyable.

The orchid yard of the Forest Department on the Imphal-Dimapur National Highway about 7 km. from Imphal is also one of the important features in Manipur. About 500 varieties of orchids including rare species are grown in Manipur and of which more than 110 varieties are grown in this orchid yard. The orchid spells love, peace and tenderness of the nature and any one who has visited the spot never forgets it. Peak season is April-May.

Eight km. down the Indo-Burma Road lies the small hill feature, Langthabal with the relics of an old palace. It offers a pleasant view of the surroundings and overlooks the Manipur University at Canchipur.

About 16 km. from Imphal on the Indo-Burma Road is Waithou, famous for its picturesque scenic spot and also famed for its pineapples.

Kaina is a hillock about 921 metres above the sea level and a sacred place of the Hindus. So goes the history that one night Shri Govindajee appeared in the vision of his royal devotee

Shri Jai Singh Maharaja (later known as Bhagyachandra of Manipur) in his dream and asked the saintly king to install in a temple an image of Shri Govindajee on the likeness of what appeared in the dream. It was to be carved out of jackfruit tree which was then growing at Kaina. The scenery is charming and the hill shrubs and natural surroundings give the place a saintly and religious atmosphere. It is only 29 km. from Imphal by bus via Thoubal. Raas Lila is performed there now and then on the particular days.

Another place worth visiting in Manipur is Pallel. It lies before the National Highway No.39 takes to the hills, at 55 km. It was here that the Officers of the Indian National Army (I.N.A.) led by Col. Swami Lakshmi Nathan kissed the soil as the first liberated area in India. From a place about 10 km. off Pallel towards Burma one gets a spectacular bird eyeview of the whole of Imphal valley.

Tengnoupal is the highest point on the Imphal-Burma Road and from here one can have a full view of the valley of Manipur. When you pass along the road you will find yourself above the clouds but in natural surroundings. It is 69 km. from Imphal in the southeast and is connected with the capital by regular bus service.

Khonigjom is a historical place and is about 37 km. from Imphal on the Imphal-Burma Road. It is here where Major-General Paona Brajabashi, one of the great warriors of Manipur, proved his valour against the superior force of the invading British Army in 1891. He laid down his life in this battlefield in defence of his motherland without turning his back to the enemy. The hillock at the foot of Khebuching, where he fell, is lovely and reminiscent of the past heroic deeds of the Manipuri warriors. The War Memorial on the top of this scenic hill feature adds charm to this historic site.

Moreh town on the Indo-Burmese border is 110 km. from Imphal in the south-east. This is the border town between India and Burma. As one enters the Burmese territory he will find the creepers winding around trees left to right while the opposite is said to be the case in the area of Manipur. It is a place of high strategic importance. A National Highway connects it with Imphal.

Rupees 100 crores Loktak Hydro Electric Project forms part of the Loktak Multipurpose Scheme which envisages power generation, irrigation facilities and reclamation of land. The project derives its name from the serenely beautiful Loktak lake, situated some 35 km. from the capital city of Imphal in the lush green valley of Manipur State, famous for its traditional heritage. Some 58'8 cumecs of water will be diverted from the lake out of which 16'8 cumecs will be utilised for the lift irrigation scheme and 43 cumecs for generation of power. With a gross head of 312 metres, the water will spin three hydro units in the power plant, each unit being of 35 MW capacity. This ambitious and comprehensive project which is so far the biggest in the region aims at economic development of Manipur and neighbouring States of North-Eastern Region. The project, after passing through many difficult situations has now been commissioned.

Bishenpur is 27 km. from Imphal on the Tiddim Road. It is a picturesque town situated at the foot of hills that roll down to the valley. The 15th century Vishnu temple built of peculiar small bricks supposedly of Chinese influence during the reign of King Kiyamba is of historical importance.

Red Hill (Lockpaching) is a hillock about 16 km. from Imphal on Tiddim Road. It is a thrilling spot where a fierce battle took place between the British and Japanese forces in the World War II and regarded as a holy place.

Moirang is one of the ancient villages of Manipur. It contributed much to her culture. It is situated about 45 km. off Imphal to the south. It was Moirang which nursed Khamba and Thoibi, traditional figures of Manipur from whom the much known Khamba-Thoibi dance originated. Moirang is also the abode of Thangjing, the most venerated deity. In his honour the traditional "Moirong Lai Haraoba" is celebrated sometime in the month of May every year since the olden days. During the festival, men and women in hundreds dance and sing in honour of Thangjing. The veriegated costumes traditionally worn on the occasion add beauty to the rhythm of dance and music. The great World War II brought Moirang into the limelight as it was, for a short spell, the headquarters of the Azad Hind Fauz. It was here that Netaji Subhash Chandra Bose hoisted for the first time the flag of I.N.A. on the Indian soil. Moirang offers INA Memorial with the statue of Netaji Subhash Chandra Bose, the replica of the monolith of Netaji at Singapore in 1945, and a small War Museum. The I.N.A. Memorial at Moirang contributes much to the tourist interest.

Loktak Lake : It is the largest fresh water lake in the North-Eastern Region. It is 45 km. from Imphal and is most enjoyable to the tourists. The vast expanse of water offers scope for shooting, fishing and boating. The aquatic birds float double on the lake. The little island of Thanga and Karang with beautiful garden resorts in the centre of the lake serve as observatories to view the majestic scenery of nature with the marvellous reflection on the water of the lake. The village belles and boatmen with oars in hand singing sweet music carry the tourists to the ends of the horizon. The angler has adequate scope to busy himself with the rod and the line in the lake. The importance of Loktak lake as tourist centre lies in its scenic beauty with islands in the centre of the vast sheet of sparkling water, its grassy margin, labyrinth of boat routes amidst the floating marshes and colourful water plants. It takes different seasonal appearances which are the real prize of tourism. The floating marshes are haunted by wild beasts and they used to be hunting places in the past. The National Park at Kaibul Lamjao deserves special mention. Particular mention may be made of the availability of the rarest species Brow Antlerd Deer in this partk, the race of which is said to have been extinct in other parts of the world.

New Churachandpur: It is on the Tiddim Road 60 km. from Imphal and is one of the most beautiful places for sightseeing and holidaying. Inhabited by the non-Naga hill tribes, it is an advanced tribal village and District Headquarters where products of arts and crafts of the area are available in local market.

Ukhrul : 83 km. from Imphal in the east and is the District Headquarters of Manipur East District. It is 1900 metres above the sea level and is the highest hill station of Manipur. It is practically as high and cold as Simla. A centre of warrior and colourful tribe of Tangkhul Nagas, it is a well developed hilly place. It is famous for a peculiar type of land-lily known as Siroi Lily grown on the Siroi hills. Siroi hill is 2456 metres high and lies in the east of Ukhrul town. Ukhrul bears the gayest and the most festive appearance during Christmas.

Koubru Hill : It is said that civilization of Manipur originated from Koubru situated on one of the highest peaks in the northern hill ranges of Manipur. According to mythology human habitation started first at Koubru and then spread all over the State and the world at large. Koubru is thus quite sacred and dear to the Manipuris and thousands visit this place to pay homage to the Koubru deity during favourable season of the year. It is pilgrim centre on the high hills.

Kangchup : Kangchup, 921 metres above sea level and 16 km. from Imphal in the west, is a health resort on the hills overlooking the Imphal Valley. The scenery is picturesque. It is a place worth seeing. It is connected with Imphal by motor service. There is an Inspection Bungalow. It is a mountain pass on road to Tamenglong.

Mao : Mao, a hill station, is half way between Imphal and Dimapur on the National Highway No. 39. It is at 106 km. and is 1788 metres high, the highest portion of the National Highway. The place is rich in Naga culture. A Mao Naga fully armed, is an object of beauty and awe. The climate is healthy and never too hot.

Time seems to compress itself in Manipur. A fragment torn from history lies in close juxtaposition with the vision of a grand national design. In this vast panorama of traditional culture seeking to coexist with modernity, the proverbial "once upon a time" is still very much alive in Manipur.

2

Manipuri Dance

Kapila Vatsyayan

MANIPURI may be described as a dance form which is at once oldest and the youngest among the classical Indian dances. In its present form, it is comparatively free, being bound only in a limited manner to the literary word and the rigidity of the *tala*. It is seemingly free and spontaneous, apparently easy and flowing. Looked at closely, this dance style is the manifestation of a deeply ritualistic tradition, combined with a vitality with which an art form throbs only when it is shared by the community at large.

There is no coherent history of the earliest inhabitants of Manipur, a jewel of natural beauty, lying amidst the hills on the north-eastern borders of India. However, there is enough evidence to prove that a rich culture flourished here even during the pre-Aryan days. The small valley and the adjoining hills contained many ethnological types, many tribes known by the generic name of the Nagas inhabit the area to this day. Without going into the ethnological complexities of the region, one might classify, for purposes of discussion, the inhabitants of the region into valley dwellers and hill people. Manipur belongs largely to the valley people who call themselves Meities and trace their antiquity to the Vedic times. Whatever the heritage, it is fairly well-established that many ritual practices were prevalent very early in the region. The continuity of such ritual practices is sustained by the dances. The ritual dances were not merely trance dances or dances for exorcising evil spirits, but were of sheer devotion and dedication to an unknown god.

The Meities as a community knew innumerable ritual dances, but the most exquisite example is the dance of the Maibas and Maibees. These priests and priestesses were the heralders of good. Clad in spotless white, they invoked the deity through repetitive but disciplined movement. Apart from this, there were the dances by couples in which the theme was a local legend of two types, Lai haraoba and Kambha Thoibi. Rather than performing before an image of a god, they danced to an abstract design which symbolized the intertwined serpent. Undoubtedly the purpose of worship was to invoke a deity who was 'formless' and is not identifiable with any known Hindu god. The abstract design was executed through concentrated movement, repetitive in character and highly symbolic in presentation.

Not until the 17th century did Hinduism, become the state religion of this secluded valley, although some form of Vaishnavism may have reached there earlier. This, of course, is conjectural but seems valid since some of the Meitie dances can be identified as based on the earlier Saivaite tradition.

Since the religious impact of Hinduism or, more, specifically, Vaishnavism was acknowledged only about the 17th century, Manipuri has been sometimes called the youngest amongest the classical dance styles of India. However, the evolution of its distinct form was the result of a mutual interaction between the earlier ritualistic dances and the Vaishnava *bhakti* cult. Thus, while today Manipuri dancing is the richest manifestation of the Vaishnavaite tradition, the distinctive form of Vaishnavism practised here is certainly a result of the super imposition of the *bhakti* cult on the area's earlier ritualistic practices.

Legend has it that, in the 18th century, a king of Manipur named Garib Niwaz formally embraced Vaishnavism although earlier there were other Hindu influences at work also. It is known that Sant Dass of Bengal had visited Manipur and that King Kahagemba had built a small temple dedicated to Vishnu. Thus, when Garib Niwaz officially declared Vaishnavism the State religion, the ground had been prepared by earlier Vaishnava missionaries. Sant Dass, however, left the deepest impact on the people. The Vaishnavism of the Chaitanya school attracted the inhabitants.

At this time, the people held ritualistic practices at their shrines (*umanglais*). With the advent of Vaishnava appeared a new structure called *Mandapas*, where Vaishnava devotional singing (*kirtan*) replaced these earlier ritual practices. The Meitie community-singing and Maibee dance gradually took the shape of the *kirtans* and the *cholams* of Vaishnavaite tradition. The various sects of Vaishnavism such as Vishnu-swami, Madhavacharya and Ramanandi contributed to the deep impact on the people. All future development of the State religion of Vaishnavism and, consequently, of its dances, was a result of these influences.

Nowhere else in India are the *rasas*, described in *Srimad Bhagavata*, so alive as in Manipur. Bit by bit, chapter by chapter, the scenes of the Bhagavata are recreated. In these *rasa* dances, a myriad moods and facets of the Krishna legend are presented in fascinating manner.

It must be remembered that although the Meities assimilated the Vaishnava tradition, the older forms and themes were never given up. The result is a rich repertoire, divided into two clear parts. The first consists of the Meitie dances, such as the Lai haraoba and the Kambha Thoibi, while the second includes the Vaishnavaite dances which chiefly present the varieties of *rasa* dances and the *bhangis*.

From the 18th century onwards, the history of the dance style can be traced fairly accurately. The present form and repertoire of the dance is attributed to another king who saw it all in a dream. It is said that King Bhagychandra Maharaja (18th century) saw in a religious trance Lord Krishna and the Gopis performing the divine dance. Both the *rasa* dances and the present costumes of Manipuri are attributed to the king's dream.

But for the recent discoveries of manuscripts in Manipuri, the tale about the dream of king could have been dismissed merely as a legend. The manuscripts are convincing evidence of the incomparable contribution of this king to the modern Manipuri dance. The Maharaja wrote a manual on dance called the *Govinda Sangita Lila Vilas*. Of course, there is some controversy about the authenticity of this text in Manipuri language but the controversy does not invalidate its importance. The treatise, roughly of the period 1774 to 1784, lays down clearly the scope of this dance style. From this work, we gather that there were also two earlier works, namely, the *Nartan Vartika* of Chitrarath Gandharva and the *Raasaprakasa* of Gargacharya, but both the works have been lost.

The *Govinda Sangita Lila Vilas* generally follows the Natyasastra tradition, but makes significant departures. In this work, he defines *tandava* and *lasya*, which are not found in the treatises of the medieval period from other parts of India. The *tandava* is divided into the *chalanam* and the *gunthanam*. *Lasya* is also subdivided into *simitanga* and *sphuritanga*. This classification is distinctive to this work and is followed to this day in contemporary practice. His classification of *Natya* also differed from the classification known to the other treatises which have only divided the generic term into *nritta*, *nritya* and *natya*. The author divides it into *rasaka* and *rupaka*. The word *rupaka* may be identified as a variant of the *dasa rupaka* and the other *natika* and *prakarana* forms of the *Natyasastra* tradition. The *rasaka* comes as something new. Although *rasa* is mentioned in the *Natyasastra*, it is not elaborately described by Bharata. The author devotes a full chapter to the *rasaka* and speaks in detail of the various types of *rasa* dances the *maharasa*, *majurasa*, *nityarasa*, *nirvesarasa* or the *kunjarasa*. He also speaks about the *goparasa* and quotes not Bharata as his authority but Gargacharya.

Judging from this description, it would appear, that, in Manipuri not only the purely sastric tradition of the *Natyasas-*

tra but also the Puranic tradition of the *Srimad Bhagavata* have been blended. An authoritative sanction is thus given to the dance. In his discussion of the various *angas* and *upangas*, we find a detailed account of the knee positions and *hastas*. Significantly, however, we do not find a minute discussion of the various facial movements which were dealt with at length in the treatises of the South, especially those in Telugu and Malayalam.

A comparison of the textual descriptions and contemporary practices reveals that, by and large, Manipuri receives its theoretical sanction from this text. The *chalis* and the *bhangis* known to the dance style, the *gatibhangas* as also the various types of *chalans* and *sthanakas* can be directly traced to this text rather than to the texts available in other parts of India.

However, this is not the only manuscript which we find in Manipur. Somewhat later, another king wrote a treatise called the *Mridanga Sangraha*. This work is attributed to Chandrakirti and contains extremely valuable details of playing the particular variety of drum called the *khol* in Manipuri. The other treatise, *Sri Krishna Raasa Sangita Sangraha* by Bhakti Siddhanta, was, perhaps, written earlier than the *Mridanga Sangraha*. It contains many of the lyrics to which the *raasa* dances are performed today.

In technique, Manipuri is a far cry from anything we know in the other styles of dance. It has a flow and a grace, which contrasts distinctively from the precision and terse clarity of the South Indian styles. This impression of ease and fluidity, which is not a negation of precision, results from an unusual treatment of the body. The vertical line of the body is never broken. There are no deflections or sharp shifts from particular horizontal *sutras* as in Orissi or in Bharatanatyam. In fact, the body merely curves itself into a figure of 8. The positions attained are thus relaxed and controlled rather than sculpturesque. An effort is made to connect two parts of the body through beautiful curves. There are no sudden transitions from one posture to another; one melts into the other.

With the figure 8 or the intertwined serpents ((*nagabandha mudra*) as a basic motif, it is no longer possible to have a spread out, open position of the lower limbs so characteristic of the South Indian styles. The knees are kept close together, flexed in front, in what may be identified as the *nata* position of the knees in the *Natyasastra* tradition. The body is held upright, but without any tension. The torso once again is not treated as a unit, but is divided into two distinct parts above the *katisutra*, the chest and the waist. Neither unit is used singly because the bend of any one part by itself would mean creating an angle. Thus, the chest and the waist, although moving in opposition, are always connected. The effect is of the slow drawing of a curve in the shape of "S", but it is never a simple bend. The neck and the head follow this principle but the head never moves horizontally as in Bharatanatyam or Kathak. Instead, it also executes a figure of 8 in space. The arms and hands follow the pattern of the lower limbs and the torso. They too are never tense nor are they ever in acute flexion. The are held, in a naturally relaxed manner, away from the body in semi-circular curve, The wrists play an extremely important part in the movement of the hands and the fingers, because it is the wrists which give the movements of the fingers a unique fluidity. A basic movement is the gradual closing in and opening out of the fingers, while the wrist attempts to execute a lateral figure of 8. The face is placid and without any exaggerated facial expressions. This controlled, but not unduly severe or austere, expression is sustained throughout the performance.

What has been described here is however restricted to the movements of the feminine type and may be described, in the language of the *Govinda Sangita Lila Vilas* as the *simitanga*. A deliberate attempt at limiting space and restricting movement is made here. In the *sphuritanga*, although greater freedom is allowed, it is once again within the definite limits set by the dancer. In the *lasya* portions, even in the *sphuritanga*, the dancer does not and cannot lift her foot away from the ground above the level of the knee. The release from the ground is invariably characterized by a sweep of the ground. a gliding movement almost touching the floor rather than a movement where the foot is lifted high above the ground.

The situation changes considerably in the *tandava* portion known for its agility, verve and high leaps, whether executed by women in the role of the child Krishna or by men in the numerous male dances of the region. The basic position in *tandava* is no longer the closed feet with knees bent in front leaving no space between them. Now there is nearly a four *tala* distance between the two feet and the knees are bent in front. Normally, this is the position of the *pungcholam* dancers who usually maintain this position practically throughout the number. In the *tandava* portions, the torso is occasionally treated as a separate unit and sidebends are frequent. There are many sitting positions and many spirals and turns known to the dance style, both in *lasya* and *tandava*. In *lasya*, the *sthanakas* or various positions once again attempt to limit space and although women dancers change the level throughout a performance, there is hardly ever much space between the two feet. In the *tandava* portions, the *sthanakas* take the form of positions known as the *vrischika karanas* of the *Natyasastra* tradition. Some of these are common to Orissi and Manipuri. There are few leg extensions in the *lasya* or the *tandava* portions. The *gunthanam* described in the *Govinda Sangita Lila Vilas* in the context of *tandava* may be identified as the various sitting and jumping movements in *tandava* when there is comparatively little distance between the feet and the knees. However, neither in the *tandava* portions nor in the *lasya* portions are hip movements allowed. There is one type of thigh or pelvic movement known to the dance style. It is an up-and-down movement rather than a side-to-side movement, with the shift of weight from one foot to the other characteristic of styles like the Orissi. The up-and-down movement is achieved through knee dips and through a suggestion of a hop on the toe.

The manner of covering space in Manipuri is expressive of its grace and delicacy. The dancer covers floor space also in figure of 8 and, when the foot is lifted to cover space, it invariably touches the ground by a slight toe movement rather than the flat foot or the heel. The *Kunchita* foot or the *agratala-sanchara* foot of the *Natyasatra* is seen repeatedly in this dance style. Many of the complex dance movements are derived from a dexterous use of the *kunchita* foot.

The dancer begins with the movements known as the *chali*. The *chali* need not be identified with the *chari* of the *Natyasastra*, but it is definitely a movement which suggests basic ways of walking and covering space. The dancer moves first to the front and back with hands held horizontally at the chest level and then moves these hands vertically in an up-and-down direction. She then covers space in a side-ways walking, ending by weaving circles and spirals. In these basic movements, the various types of *bhramaris* are introduced, the two distinct varieties being the *uplai* and the *longlai*. The *uplai* and the *longlai* have been identified by some scholars as the *bahva bhramari* and *antara bhramari* of the *Natyasastra*. We may understand these *lais* whether in *lasya* or in *tandava* as ways of covering floor space ; usually, it is side-ways movement followed by a semi-circle. They are the finale of the dance cadences and are often executed in multiples of three as in the *tihai* of the other dance styles. Sometimes, a spiral movement in vertical space is executed, where the dancer treats her body like a screw and weaves a spiral vertically from a higher level to lower level. While doing so, the dancer also takes a circle or a spin. This very difficult movement has a graceful fluidity, sometimes mistaken for imprecision. The *achongba* or jumping movements are characteristic of the *tandava* portions of the dance.

The basic movements of the *chali* are connected together to form the various typs of *parengs*. The *parengs* are perhaps parallel to the *tirmanams* of Bharatanatyam for they are cadences of movement in a given metrical cycle. The metrical cycles are very many and the in-beats are complicated, requiring a high sense of precision. All the *lais* are used in *parengs* and different types of *talas* are employed, especially the *rajmela*, 7 beats (*rupaka*), the

15 beats (*panchamsavari*) and the 16 beats (*tintala*). Three *bhangis* are attributed to King Bhagyachanda Maharaja and two to his descendant, King Chandrakiriti. The first three *bhangis*, the *bhangi pareng achongba*, the *vrindavan pareng*, and the *Khurumba pareng* are known as the *lasya* cadences. They are used in the *rasa* portions of the dance. The three other *bhangis* have a common adjective *gostha* which stands for the *tandava bhangis*. They are used by actors while presenting the character of Krishna in the *rasa* dances. Three such *bhangis* are prescribed, namely, the *gostha bhangi pareng*, the *gostha vrindavan pareng*, and the *gostha khurumba pareng*. The last one is rarely performed and seems to have gone out of vogue.

With such an elaborate system, it is not surprising that the dance has a highly complex technique of movement and *tala*. The dance is not restricted to solo numbers. Manipuri is perhaps the only classical style in which we find exquisite survivals of compositions, such as the *hallisaka*, the *charchari* and other forms mentioned in classical Sanskrit literature. Group formations mentioned in the *Natyasastra* have been lost to other classical forms. One comes across some survivals in folk forms, but Manipuri exhibits, in a well-chiselled fashion, the many types of *pindibandhas* described in the *Natyasastra*. In the *rasa* dances, we find that all the four types of *pindis* mentioned by Bharata can be seen. We also see that other group formations mentioned in later texts find a place in the different numbers of the Manipuri dance.

It is not easy to discuss the repertoire of Manipuri dance because it demands a definition of Manipuri as a classical style. Innumerable folk styles are prevalent and a large variety of community dances are still practised, besides a sizeable number of ritualistic dances known to the region. It is, therefore, somewhat erroneous to limit a discussion of the repertoire merely to the *rasa* dances of Manipur.

First and foremost are the survivals of the ritual dances which have been absorbed into the repertoire. The *Lai Haraoba* and the *Khamba Thoibi* may be counted amongst these. The

Shri Jawaharlal Nehru
giving away prizes
to Manipur Contingent

Prime Minister Smt. Indira Gandhi with folk dancers

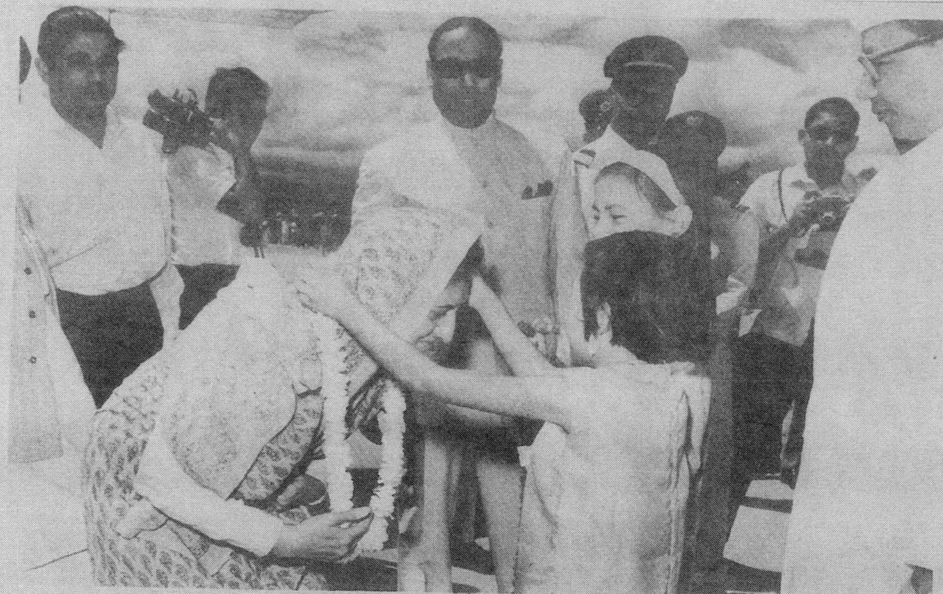

Smt. Indira Gandhi being garlanded on her arrival at Imphal

Smt. Indira Gandhi
addressing in Imphal

Polo game being played in Imphal

Wrestling in Manipuri style

Folk dancers of Manipur in Delhi

Raslila of Manipur

Manipuri couple singing a bhajan

Folk dancers at Rajpath in New Delhi on Republic Day

Smt. Indira Gandhi with Manipuri women
at Raj Bhavan, Imphal

Indian National Army Stupa in Imphal

Folk dancers of Manipur

A Manipuri girl in a bridal dress

Statue of Netaji at the Indian National Army Martyrs Memorial Ground unveiled by Shri V.V. Giri, then President of India

Shri V.V. Giri inaugurates
the Martyrs Memorial Stupa.

historical and mythical theme makes them as classical as any of the later Vaishnavaite dances. They have an element of *abhinaya* besides pure *nritta*. It is true that the relationship of the "word" and the "gesture" is neither so precise nor so formalistic as in the other classical dances. However, since the element exists and since there is a definite pattern of movement, it would not be wrong to include these numbers in a discussion of the classical repertoire.

There are then the various types of *cholams* and the different varieties of the *Kartalis*. The *cholams* are both *lasya* and *tandava*. Those belonging to the feminine group are the *cholams* of the small cymbals, namely, the *kanjira cholam* and those of the *tandava* type are the *kartala cholam* with large cymbals. The dance of the *khol* which is performed by men, may be said to be the highest achievement. The dance may be executed by a solo performer or by a hundred men. The range of sound which can be produced through the *pung* has to be experienced to be believed. Perhaps, among percussion instruments, there is no other *mridanga* which can command the same range of communicative sound as the *pung*.

There are other *cholam* dances too, such as the duff *cholam* and the *kanjira cholam*. Amongst the *kartali* dances are the clapping items performed only by women known as the *nupi khumbak ishai* and the *nupa khumbak ishi*. These are group dances in which a number of interesting group formations can be seen and the dance is built on clapping of hands at cross rhythms to the basic rhythm played by the accompanying *pung*. All the *cholam* and the *kartali* dances are pure *nritta*. There is no *abhinaya*, nor is there any song accompaniment.

To the *cholam* and the *kartali* dances must be added another variety of *tandava* dancing in the region, namely, the *thang haiba* and the *takhew saiba* or the sword and the spear dances. These are vaguely reminiscent of the *kalis* of Kerala and are purely martial dances.

Strictly speaking, all these dances are on the margin of classical and folk dances. They are invariably performed in groups and are known to the community at large. Although one soloist or a group of people may attain a high degree of perfection, they are dependent for their success on group participation. The accompanying music is recurrent and refrains are typical.

It is only when we come to the *rasa* dances that the richness of both *nritt abhinaya* of the Manipuri style can be seen. Here, we find that the art attains the same level of perfection and stylization as any of the other developed dance drama forms of India. These are compositions of a high literary order set to classical music and performed to a given metrical cycle. Bhagyachandra Maharaja is said to be the composer of at least three of the four *rasa* dances known to Manipur. There is the *Vasanta rasa* for the full-moon day of Holi, and the *Kunja rasa* which is performed on the *Rakhi-Purnima* in August. The third is the *Maha rasa* which is performed on full-moon day of the *kartika Purnima* in October-November. King Chandrakiriti added the *Nitya rasa*, and possibly the *gopa rasa*. The *rasa* dances follow a very definite pattern which gives full scope for solo dancing, for *pas de deux* and for the *core de ballet*. In the *Kunja rasa*, for example, there is the sequence of Radha entering first discovering that Krishna has danced with another *sakhi* ; this is followed by the dance of Krishna and the other *sakhis*, then comes the *abhisara* of Radha and finally the union of Krishna and Radha. Another *rasa* begins with the Krishna *abhisara* followed by the Radha *abhisara*, followed by group *rasalila* and the union of Radha and Krishna, culminating in the *prarthana*.

The literature of these *rasa* dances is Vaishnavaite, but at the same time it gives full scope to the actors to present the various *nayikas* of the Indian aesthetic tradition and the several *sthayibhavas* mentioned in *Natyasastra*. In all these, through the various episodes of the *rasa* a dominant mood (rasa) which is usually *karuna* is created. Through the presentation of the transitory states, a configuration is produced of a dominant state of being. If the concept of *rasotpatti* is to be experienced one must go to Manipur and watch a full presentation of the *Maha rasa*. Through each sequence the dancers present innumerable transitory states (vyabhicharibhavas). The various cadence of the *bhangis* give the fullest scope to the dancer to present variations on a given metrical theme.

The *rasa* dances thus constitute the most significant portion of the Manipuri repertoire. Other compositions known to this dance style are usually the songs of Jayadeva from the *Gita Govinda* or *Vidyapati's Padavali* or the works of other poets of the *Bhakti* school. Often, these lyrics are woven into the *rasa* dances. It is only a recent practice that in presenting short numbers, these *padas* are performed as *Gitabhinaya* separately. When the dancer performs the portions of *pareng*, she is known to do *nritta* on just the mnemonics (bols) called the *mukhaboli*. Some other musical compositions like the *tanum* and the *Gitabhava* have also been employed by dancers, but they do not constitute an essential part of the Manipuri repertoire.

The dance of Krishna and the cowherds forms yet another group where instead of the Krishna-Radha theme, only an episods of the playful Krishna is presented. The two *goshta bhangis* along with the numbers known as *gostha nartana* or the *gopa rasa* complete the repertoire of Manipuri dancing. Many episodes of the playful Krishna are presented ; it may be the episodes of killing the demon Bakasure or the story of the playful child stealing butter. The *vatsalya bhava* is predominant in these numbers and one finds that very often the same mood of sheer ecstasy is created through these numbers as it is in some of the numbers of Bharatanatyam where this aspect of Krishna's life is presented. These episodes are enacted by the dancer impersonating Krishna rather than a narration by Yashoda of his pranks as in Bharatanatyam. The aim is the same, that is, to present the ambivalencc of the human attitude to this child-god. Whatever the path, they really lead to the same thing because, ultimately, the actor who enacts the role either of Krishna, or Yashoda, or *gopis*, or any other character in these dances represents humanity looking up, yearning for identity with the Godhead.

The permeating mood which Manipuri dance evokes is that of devotion, deep yearning and *karuna*. It symbolizes the pangs of separation from the Godhead, the reunion with Divinity and in the last analysis, all humans are *gopis*, ever seeking, ever desiring, ever yearning for the God who gives the illusion of being personal to each human being and is yet above them all. The description in *Srimad Bhagavata* of the *rasa* is not only enacted here but permeates the very spirit of the dance.

As a theatre spectacle, Manipuri has a delicate grace and beauty. It is full of the intricate complexities of sinuous curves. In theme and spirit, it is the embodiment of *Bhakti* at its purest.

3

Martial Arts

E. Nilakanta Singh

MANIPUR is synonymous with dance to the world outside. Her colourful and rhythmic dances, both traditional and classical, need no introduction, but the rich heritage of martial arts which constitutes a significant area of the culture of the people is not so well known. Only recently, a few popular specimens of the martial arts, of the style of "sword and spear" dances, have been seen to the surprise and excitement of many. These are composed dances, movements made to order, and they have a beauty and charm of their own. There is also wrestling, Manipuri style, which appears to have some affinity with the Mongolian style, which is invariably a part of every *Lai-Haraoba* festival. The best wrestler called *Jatra* is crowned with prizes and shown special favours.

The history of Manipur is studded with fights. Battles amongst the native chieftains and against enemies like the Burmese and the Chinese were frequent. The brave rulers of Manipur reigned supreme till they lost their freedom in the fight against the British in 1857. The Manipuris, properly speaking, the Meiteis, are a martial race. Fighting for honour and justice is in their blood. A particular old Manipuri book, *Chainaron*—accounts of fights—recounts bouts between the commoners noted for their courtesy and sense of honour.

Fatalists as these people were, they regarded bouts of fighting with weapons as ordeals to be decided by God. When an unarmed man was challenged, he could fetch his arms and fix a date for the contest. Sometimes, in spear bouts, the two rivals measured out a distance acceptable to both with their spears, and standing at fixed points, hurled spears against each other. It was a point of honour to surrender the first choice. A slight scratch was sufficient for acknowledging defeat and the loser would allow his head to be chopped off in good grace. Such was the code of honour that sometimes the victor and the vanquished would share a meal together and enjoy wine in a sporting spirit, before the latter was beheaded. These tales of Manipuri heroism and chivalry inspired the people for generations to withstand all possible attacks. Vaishnavism with its accent on humility has made the people soft and refined for the last two centuries. But scratch a Manipuri and you will still find the warrior in him. Visions and traditions die hard.

Manipur has a rich repertoire of manly sports like polo, the Manipuri style of hockey, and of wrestling. But let us take three types of martial arts for a close look—sword fights, spear fights and Manipuri wrestling. These are not, strictly speaking, "performing arts". They are serious forms of self-defence, even acts of aggression against the enemy in times of war. They have been metamorphosed into graceful, exciting martial arts on the modern stage. These may be called "sword and spear" dances in the style of performing arts.

The writing of the cultural history of Manipur is still in its infancy. Research is still going on and the solution to some of the problems clearly demands extensive acquaintance with the different cultures of south-east Asia, even of Tibet and China. But one thing is certain. Manipur clearly belongs to the *Tantric* belt of northern and north-eastern India, and most of the old texts in Manipuri script and old prayers too, offer glimpses into the world of Shaivism and *Tantric* cults. Even the name of the region, Manipur, might possibly have something to do with the *Manipur Chakra* of *Kundalini Yoga*, from the *Mahabharata* age.

But what is *Tantra* ? *Tantra* means that which spreads. As one practises it, it develops more and more. Long after the *Vedic* civilisation passed away, there was a movement to reclaim and revive the old heritage. The *Brahmanas* were devoted to the study of rituals and ceremonies while the *Upanishads* were concerned with the pursuit of knowledge. That which revived, continued and enlarged esoteric practices was termed *Tantra*. There are many "lines" of *Tantra*, many forms of *Tantra*. But common to all, as the Sadhok M. P. Pandit said, is a basic statement of the *Tantric* conception of God, Nature and Man. There is one Reality which cannot be described or defined; it is supreme, absolute, it is what is called *parashiva* the transcendent. That reality is self-existent. When the *parashiva* has the mood to manifest, there is a vibration called *spanda*. It becomes Shiva and Shakti, the static consciousness and the dynamic consciousness.

The *Tantra Yoga* looks upon the human body as a miniature universe. Just as there is a divine consciousness in the universe, so there is the same consciousness in the human body also. But this consciousness is ruled by ignorance and falsehood. To recover the true consciousness, *Tantra* provides many disciplines, chiefly three; (1) the Deity, the Godhead, (2) the form, either a *murti* or a diagram in the form of a circle or a triangle—"a *yantra* or a configuration of forces represented by the Deity", (3) *mantras*, certain words or syllables which constitute the "aural" emanation of the Deity.

According to an old tradition in Manipur, the use of a spear or a sword with certain steps is associated with the creation of the world. The Lord asked His eldest son to create the world and on the request of the son, opened His mouth and showed him the world of nerves inside. He asked His son to create the same pattern outside, which he did with the help of nine gods and seven goddesses who were created out of Him. This is a *Puranic* episode, allied to the world of *Tantras*, having the microcosm linked with the macrocosm.

Thengou : the first steps of creation

This pattern of the gods and goddesses is styled *Thengou*, a sacred ritualistic movement which the dancer with a sword or a spear executes on the symbolic head of a thousand-petalled lotus or on the thousand-hooded Ananta Snake, called *Pakhangba* in Manipuri. It normally admits of nine kinds as below :

Akao Thengou, on account of vigorous thrusts

Leiphal Thengou, owing to stamping by jumps

Nongphal Thengou, stamping by turns

Leichai Thengou, from stamping by feet jumping in or out

Leikak Thengou, from carefully treading the ground

Leinet Thengou, owing to stamping the earth by turning round and round

Langkak Thengou, from touching the ground with shakes and care

Akham Thengou, from a special type of movement, which was danced by kings in succession

Leishit Thengou, on account of touching extensively the earth.

The nine styles of *Thengou* have corresponding days in a week, and prosperity, war, hunger or peace is indicated by the concluding type of *Thengou*, the particular spots in the *yantra* diagram or certain areas of the snake.*kundalini*. Any mistake on the part of the performer would lead to serious misfortune to the country and, for this reason, it has been kept a secret for centuries, an exclusive art revealed only to a select few by the great masters. On certain rare occasions, the former kings of Manipur used to dance *Thengou* under the strict supervision of the *gurus* and the priests. It is now almost a dying art, hardly demonstrated on pain of inviting a curse upon the performer or the people if any mistake occurs.

It is now evident that *Thengou* is a *Tantric sadhana*, a way of prayer, a medium of communication of forces, good or evil. Of these, *Akham Thengou* is believed to bring prosperity and peace to land. Tradition says that this very *Thengou* was performed by Akhom Mayon during the reign of King Khagemba of Manipur (1597-1652), by Apong Sarotkhaiba and Thonglen Wangkheirakpa, during the reign of King Garibniwaz (1709-1748), and by Wangkhei Pandit Gopiram during the time of Rajarshi Bhagyachandra (1764-1789). Every performance of *Thengou*, whether with spear or sword, must be accompanied by the incantation of specific *mantras*.

Nine and seven are sacred numbers to the Manipuris. As in the case of the nine *Thengourols*, the art of spear dance *Ta Khousarol* also admits of nine kinds and shares the same myths and symbols as *Thengourol*. The only difference is that *Ta Khousarol* is a little more secular, more agile. The names of *Khousarol* are : *Maram Nungshitpa*, *Maram Achouba*, *Maram Macha*, *Maram Nungjongba*, *Kabui*, *Athou Chumthang*, *Athou Macha*, *Tangkhul*, *Athou Achouba* and *Thel*. Maram is a place name of the hills and Tangkhul and Kabui belong to Naga tribes. It is likely that these art forms have something to do with the tribals and the hills of Manipur. There are other types of *Khousarol* which are composed by various experts and handed down from generation to generation. These are used in the *Kwak Jatra* festival (*Dussehra*) and *Lai-Haraoba* before large audience and in the open area. Every *Khousarol* has a fixed sequence and demands great skill and agility on the part of the performer. There are also solo or duet items done as a part of the ritual and prayer for prosperity. Unlike *Thengourol* it is still an active form and practised by *gurus* and experts. An analysis of the sequence of a particular *Khousarol* would reveal the different stages in the matter of hunting and catching wild animals through artistic jumps and thrusts of spear.

The sword generally goes with the spear, and mastery of both the arts was a must for every warrior worth the name in Manipur. The spear has many shapes and is used for specific purposes like guarding the king, hunting the tiger or the elephant. Each type of spear has a name. Similarly, different types and shapes of swords belong to specific clans, various ancestors and even deities, having distinctive names. Even the royal swords have specific names like Khoubomba of King

Khagemba (1597-1652), Vajra Singh of King Gambheer (1825-1834), and Chandrasen of Maharaja Chandrakirti (1834-1844).

Every warrior versed in the use of the spear has to enter the battle-field with three types of spears—the *hakthang ta* (attached to the body), the *chaina ta* (fighting spear) and the *taaron ta* (the additional spear) kept generally on the back. The shield has to be attached to it. The expert swordsman has to carry, besides the *chungoi* (shield), three types of swords such as the *vetthang* (the right hand sword), *oithang* (the left hand one) and *tendong thang* (the additional sword) kept on the back and used like an arrow in times of emergency.

The art of sword fighting, apart from its having various steps and movements in Manipuri names, has, at the moment, corresponding non-Manipuri terms like *valak*, *kalak*, and *shut* and it is likely that this art has been influenced and enriched by a similar art of fencing in northern India. But it still preserves its distinctive character and admits of specific steps and jumps. An expert swordsman holding two swords could cover himself with the swords and protect himself against possible attacks from outside. Unfortunately, owing to incessant fights among princes of royal blood, there were times when this art was discouraged. During the British times, of course, there was a complete ban on the teaching of the martial arts, due to their policy of subjugating warrior races. But now this old art is being revived again.

There has been a fashion of increasing popularity to present this art of sword and spear on the stage as performing arts, mostly in the form of 'decorative pieces' or 'composed' fights. The way the performers take to this presentation in all seriousness clearly indicates that this is not just a dance form for enjoyment but a study in movements full of surprise and excitement. Even though the contestants agree on some basic movements, there is considerable room for improvisation. This means that no two fights, unlike the codified movements of the dance, are similar and each has a beauty and excitement of its own. It is indeed indicative of serious training of high standards that some of the presentations of sword fights, sword versus spear fights, and sword versus axe fights have been raised to heights of excellence and artistry, to the great delight of the spectators. Real fights cannot obviously be sponsored in the style of boxing or wrestling as the risks are immense. But these stage fights do not lack the seriousness, agility and artistry of the real fights and hence the beauty of the presentation sometimes eclipses the performances of traditional art forms.

Even though the classical dance forms of Manipuri claim affinity with the *Natya Shastra* and *Abhinaya Darpana* tradition, it has been increasingly proved that the steps, gaits and the poses of sword and spear dances have contributed to the framework of some of the classical forms such as the *Lai-Haraoba*, *Ras Leela* and *Sankirtana* movements. For instance *chakra hastas* of both hands, which is a must for martial arts, are used in *Lai-Haraoba* and *Ras* movements. The various poses and vigorous moves of *Pung cholom* also betray certain basic poses of sword fight. Even the basic movements like *chali*, *longlei*, and *uplei* (*bhramari*), *champra okpi*, and *lasing kappi* have been demonstrated as having some affinity to the steps and poses of martial arts. It is no wonder that some of the exponents of Manipuri music and dance make a plea for a sound knowledge of martial arts before the art of dance is studied and mastered. This, of course, does not mean that a good swordsman is necessarily a skilled dancer. It is a matter of sharing a specific vision of beauty born of movements and steps integrated to a certain ethnic group.

It would not be doing justice to the martial arts of Manipur, if *Mukna*—wrestling Manipuri style—is not included in a study of Manipuri dance forms. This is an art of self-defence with bent bodies poised against each other with hands clutching the tops of thighs by the clothes and following certain rigid rules governing the art. There is no ritual or myth behind it. It is pure sport done in a competitive manner on the lawns before the village audience, which it is the privilege of every youth to master and exhibit.

The introduction is executed with a certain amount of grace. The two contenders first bow to each other and with bent bodies move slowly but steadily towards each other till the expert or the judge arranges the hands of the contestants at their appointed places. Then the contest starts. There are only a few basic thrusts and leaps associated with this art, but its mastery demands practice and perseverance of a high order; the specialist of a particular form is always a terror to others.

In the village sports, held mostly during the *Lai-Haraoba* festival, there are a series of wrestling challenges which go on for days and even nights and the ultimate victor is crowned with the title *Jatra* and receives robes and prizes. Occasionally, challenges are thrown by the *Jatra* of one village to the that of another and it is indeed a great sight to watch both engaged and locked in Manipuri wrestling for the prestige and honour of the village.

There appears to be some resemblance between the Mongolian style of wrestling and that of Manipur. For want of proper study and research, it is too early to say anything definite about this affinity. But as a group of the Mongoloid race, the Meiteis have something to do with the art of the Mongolian people. It is more than likely that Manipur gave some of its grace and artistry to this particular form of sport or fight. But such is the beauty of this art that it is not an uncommon sight to watch a weakling, specialised in a particular form of *Mukna*, defeating a strong man with a bulky body through sheer skill in the art.

Now that there has been a revival of interest in these distinctive arts, it is safe to predict that its future is bright. Schools and institutes all over the valley of Manipur, run on a modest scale, are being established. But much more has to be done by the Government and the people to provide the proper atmosphere for the culture of these art forms of the sword, the spear and Manipuri wrestling. National institutes have to be sponsored and much of the survey and research has to be encouraged so that these may be presented on a national and even international level. A few performers have shown something remarkable on the stage outside Manipur and even India. But it is time that troupes of Manipur martial arts are presented all over India and abroad with a view to projecting an image of the ethnic culture of the Manipuris, providing a glimpse of the rich and fantastic heritage of a people deeply rooted in *Tantric* culture and a great civilisation which is India.

4

Manipuri Language

N. Tombi Singh

A BOOK, which attempts at giving some glimpses of Manipur, cannot be complete without a reference to the role of language in the development of Manipuri culture. It is a well-known fact that Manipuri is the lingua-franca of the entire population. It has also been mentioned that during the British days many of the official transactions and documents were done in Manipuri. In the Manipur Constitution Bill, passed and enforced on the eve of Manipur's integration with Indian Union, provided that Manipuri will be the official court language of the State. Mention has also been made earlier that at present all the deliberations in the Manipur Legislative Assembly and the proceedings in the courts are in Manipuri, but the proceedings are recorded in English. This is because Manipuri has not been made, through proper legislation, the official language of the State. It may be understood from the above circumstances that the case for de-jure recognition of Manipuri, the de-facto official language of the State, is tremendously strong.

The development of the language, for modern literature and for the purposes of official and academic spheres, requires future examination. So also the historical background and the treasure of early literary attainments of the language have to be opened for a critical analysis and conclusion. Over and above that, the other aspects pertaining to the fulfilment of the legitimate aspiration of this language in the present context have to be scrutinised with due emphasis. Generally, issues relating to the future and status of the provincial languages in the country are tackled more with emotion and sentiment than reason and dispassionate academic approach. This applies to both protagonists and antagonists of that language. The approach in respect of Manipuri language, however, has been as dispassionate as possible. The reader may be rest assured that no attempt is being made at establishing a claim which cannot be justified by the approved yardsticks on the subject.

Manipuri has a very scientific system of scripts. The earlier writings are in the old Manipuri scripts. How old are these scripts is for the scholars on the subject to assess. But it is generally accepted that these are considerably old and compare favourably with any other old script of the world. During the period of transition from the unmixed Manipuri tradition to the new blending of the Manipuri and Hindu traditions, the richness of the literary wealth of Manipur was discovered. Heaps of ancient manuscripts which formed the backbone of the Manipuri traditions and folklore were burnt at the instigation of the Brahmin missionaries. This occasion had two aspects, namely, discovery of the realself of Manipur and the adventure of the missionaries for extension of their cultural and literary empire. The present Manipuri society is a gift of this compromise. The old manuscripts covered almost all important aspects of human life. They throw tremendous light on every branch of science which has a relevance to human civilisation. The results of the latest drives for collection of these ancient manuscripts, at different levels, have shown beyond doubt that the ancient literary treasure of Manipur can stand comparison with any literary group in the world. The collections so far made and exhibited will speak for themselves. The only handicap is that printing in the Manipuri scripts has not been introduced.

The knowledge of the old script is confined to a small section of the population who have taken pains to learn it so that they can have access to the ancient treasure. Vigorous attempts have, however, been made to transcribe the books into Bengali script which is now used as the official script for the modern Manipuri language. The introduction of Bengali script in the Manipuri language is very recent. It started with the British conquest of Manipur. This had ample justification and led to useful openings in the spheres of printing of Manipuri literature without having to invest for setting up of separate Manipuri type foundries. For the satisfaction of sentiment and self-respect, however, the demand continues to grow for replacement of the Bengali script by Manipuri. It is very difficult to say the last word on the subject as the controversy over this issue is becoming acrimonious in some serious quarterses.

Coming to the development of Manipuri as a modern Indian language the following points deserve special attention :—

(a) It is the medium of instruction and examination upto the eighth class in the whole of Manipur. Option is given to those whose mother tongue is not Manipuri to write in English or any other Indian language.

(b) Manipuri as an elective subject has been introduced upto degree classes.

(c) Arrangements are being made to open M.A. in Manipuri in some Universities.

(d) The issue of making the language medium of instruction and examination upto Matriculation is awaiting early finalisation.

(e) Manipuri has been recognised as a Modern Indian Language by the Sahitya Akademi.

(f) A bibliography of modern publications in the language has been prepared by the Manipuri Sahitya Parishad. The same has shown that the subjects covered in the publications are many and varied. The depth and the extent of this coverage can be compared with any modern Indian language.

The publications include original works and translations from leading works in English, Sanskrit and other Indian languages. Authentic dictionaries and works on grammar and history of the language have been published in large numbers. The translations include those from the immortal epics, the *Mahabharata* and the *Ramayana.* The translation from the *Mahabharata* is a big project which will cover twenty-three big volumes of nearly five hundred pages each. So far eighteen volumes have been published. The translator, Sri Kalachand Shastri, a distinguished Sanskrit scholar, was awarded Padmashri by the President of India for his valuable contribution in this behalf.

(g) In recognition of the achievements of the language, the Gauhati University has opened a separate section for Manipuri books in the University Library.

Special mention may be made here of the contribution made to the enrichment of Modern Manipuri Literature by translations of distinguished Bengali poets and writers like Rabindranath Tagore, Bankimchandra, Sarat Chandra Chatterjee and others, besides those from Shakespeare and other prominent English writers.

Among original works are Dr. Kamal's 'Madhabi' a novel, and Hijam Angahal's 'Khamba Thoibi Sheireng', an epic poem which runs into about thirty thousand lines. Among other modern writers and poets mention may be made of Khwairakpam Chaoba. Arambam Dorendra, Hawaibam Nabadwip, Minaketan, Nilakanta, G.C. Tongbra, Shitaljit, Nilbir Shastri, A. Shyamsundar, Shurchand Sarma, Hijam Guno, M.K. Binodini, Thoibi Rajanikanta, Kunja Mohan, Samarendra, Khumanthem Ibohal, Sanjenbam Nadia, Lourembam Ibungoyaima, Haobam Ibungoyaima. Ananda Mohan, Sonamani, Irengbam Gulamjat, Dr. Ibotonsa and Thangjam Chaoba.

The demand for inclusion of Manipuri in the Eighth Schedule of the Constitution has been voiced by all political parties and leading literary and cultural organisations in Manipur for the last several years. It is one of the basic aspirations of the people. With the conferment of fulfledged Statehood to Manipur one of the basic aspirations of the people has been fulfilled. This has to be followed by inclusion of Manipuri in the Eighth Schedule, and a vigorous programme of economic development. The emphasis here is on the legitimate right of Manipuri to be in the Eighth Schedule as the language of a State.

The leadership of the country who has shown unparallelled wisdom in the reorganisation of North-Eastern Areas will not take much time in taking the much needed decision in this behalf.

About the basic character and origin of Manipuri language a few lines could be added. The language falls within the Mongolian Group and has thus practically no basic affinity with Sanskrit or any language worth mentioning. But the cultural and religious contact with the rest of India for several centuries has made a significant impact on the development of Manipuri as an Indian language. A large number of technical terms and popular Sanskrit vocabularies has crept into the vocabulary structure of the language. It is, therefore, becoming easier and easier day by day for a non-Manipuri, with some background of Sanskrit or any other Indian languages which have Sanskrit vocabularies, to learn Manipuri. This factor has its disadvantage in respect of the hill tribes who have embraced Christianity, thereby estranging themselves from the mainstream of Indian linguistic current. They complain that they are more at home with pure and archaic Manipuri than with the Sanskritised one. In order to bring the tribal belts within the mainstream of Indian culture and language, adequate measures have to be taken up, specially in the sphere of education and through the medium of mass education and information. This will not only help the tribal Christians in catching up with the modern trend of Sanskritisation in the Manipuri language but also will bring them closer to Indian mainstream of thought and culture. Nevertheless writers of text books in Manipuri for the hill areas have to appreciate the real difficulties of the hill people in this behalf.

Some of the tribal dialects have proved their suitability and justification for development, upto certain stage, for the purposes of education. Three dialects have come up for such development from the Naga group of the hill people. They are Kabui, Mao and Tankhul. These dialects have already received the attention of the All India Radio. Akashvani Imphal has given them prominent place among dialects used as medium of its broadcast in the region. The selection of suitable dialects among the Kukis or non-Naga group for adequate development appears to be full of problems. These problems arise out of the fact that each of sub-tribes in this group likes to push up its dialect to be the selected one. If it would have been possible to patronise all of them for use as educational medium upto higher levels, the problems would have been lessened. The dialects of the Kuki group with certain minor variations here and there are more or less of the same origin and structure. Members of any two different sub-tribes in the Kuki group can understand one another while each speaking his own dialect. The real solution in this regard appears to lie in making the component tribes to agree to a certain reasonable compromise so that they could develop a dialect into a really workable modern Indian language for the purpose of their education. The neighbouring Union Territory of Mizoram has Lusai as its language. Lusai is treated as one of the modern Indian languages for the purpose of education. The Kuki group of the tribals in Manipur is quite at home in Lusai. They, therefore, take up this language in the course of their studies, whenever they are required to take up a modern Indian language and upto that extent Lusai can serve the purpose.

The new state of Manipur shall have to apply its mind to the development of Manipuri as the language of the State and some selected dialects for academic purposes. A comprehensive programme has to be drawn up to meet this urgent need of the region.

5

Literature

Jyotirmoy Roy

THE Manipuris have a language of their own with a growing literature. It was first recognised as one of the vernaculars upto B.A. by the Calcutta University in the early Thirties. In 1972 for the first time a Department of Manipuri was established in the Jawaharlal Nehru University Centre at Imphal for Post-graduate studies in Manipuri literature. Earlier to that Sahitya Akademi accorded its recognition to Manipuri as one of the major Indian languages. Dr. Griesrson has placed the Manipuri language in the Kuki-chin branch of the Tibeto-Burmese family of languages. Once it had a separate script which is long out of use. Bengali script is used for writing books in Manipuri language. Attempts are now being made to bring the old script into use again.

Manipuri literature has three periods of development viz. (1) the ancient period, from the remote past to the end of the seventeenth century ; (2) The medieval period from the eighteenth century to the first quarter of the twentieth century ; and (3) the modern period which began from the end of the first quarter of the twentieth century.

The earliest gem in Manipuri literature is 'Ougri' composed in verse comparable only to the Vedic hymns in quality and purpose. The theme commemorates the incidents connected with the creation of the universe. It was recited at the coronation ceremony of Nongda Lairen Pakhangba, the founder of the ruling family of Manipur. Since then, it became customary to recite 'Ougri' during every coronation. It is also sung with suitable changes either for wishing prosperity of the kingdom or for the destruction of the enemy. It is a poem of considerable length with an impressive description of the splendour of the Sun. The importance of 'Ougri' lies in its incantory merit. 'Khencho' is the other archaic compsition. It is sung in chorus in 'Laiharaobo Festival'. So also is 'Sana Lamok', sung to evoke the spirit of Pakhangba, the presiding deity of the Meiteis. Numit Kappa (shooting the Sun), an old composition has in it much of skill and subtlety. But 'Panthoibi Khongul' definitely bears a testimony of the creative faculty of the writer of that ancient period. In it the gradual evolution of Panthoibi from a frolicking damsel to a nymph and eventually to the all-pervading spirit of the Divine Mother has been successfully traced with the fluidity of language and the height of imagination. 'Hijan Hirae' is a beautiful example of attributing human feelings to the objects of nature. The poet is deeply moved by the feelings of a mother tree whose grown-up son, a very tall tree, has been selected by the king's men for making a royal barge. Learned men and skilled carpenters have already selected the tree for the purpose and performed the necessary rituals. It will be cut down on the following day. The helpless mother observed and understood. At night she broke into wails filling the whole hillside in deep grief. Besides these longer poems, there are numerous lyrics, folk songs and ballads on a variety of themes which really display the richness of old poetry in rhyme, meter and imagery. Works in prose also went almost hand in hand with poetry. 'Poi-rieiton Khunthokpa', an account of an immigrant in that ancient period is a specimen of perfect prose. He is stated to have participated in the coronation of Nongda Lairen Pakhangba.

The style of writing in this book is different from that of

'Cheitharol Kumbaba' which is taken to be the earliest recorded chronicle of Manipur. 'Nongdan Ponbi Luwaba' is the story of a hero (named after the title of the book) who brought back the soul of his departed wife by physically over-powering the agent of the god of death. The language of 'Khongjomnubi Nonggarol' is archaic but not difficult to understand the meaning. The work is based on a legend of six girls who had been forsaken by their parents for marrying persons not recommended by them. These girls ultimately reached heaven and turned into Poleids. 'Leithak Leikharol', another notable work of this period narrates beautifully the story of the creation of the earth. Besides these works of pure literary merit there are books dealing with various subjects like historical events, philosophy, origin of clans, medicine, minerals, warfare, administration, duties of kings and laymen, flowers and orchids, the art of digging canals etc. It appears that the ancient writers were equally adept in prose as they were in verse. But none of these works prior to the eighteenth century i.e. Pre-Gharib Niwaz period bears either any date of composition or name of the author. It is explained that according to the prevalent guild system the credit of any work done by any member of the guild would go to his guild and not to the individual. That is why the ancient writers preferred to remain anonymous in their works.

Introduction of Vaishnavism in Manipur in the first quarter of the eighteenth century initiated a new course in the Manipuri literature. During the reign of Maharaja Bhagyachandra Singh, Gaudya Vaishnavism became the creed of the Manipuri Hindus. This brought them into intimate contact with the medieval Bengali Vaishnava literature. Religious sentiment, royal patronage and the effort of the Brahmins gave the Bengali language an important place in Manipur. It is found to be used in the official letters of Manipur addressed to the British Government of India. Some Manipuri poets composed devotional songs in Bengali. 'Dharani Samhita', a historical work of the period of Maharaja Gambhir Singh was written by a Manipuri in Bengali. Till 1924 Bengali continued to be the medium of instruction in schools. At that time Bengali dramas were frequently staged in Manipur. Even now the *Ramayana* of Krittibash and the *Mahabharata* of Kashiramdas, the *Chaitanya Charitamrita* and other religious literature in Bengali are read by the older generation with great devotion. Bengali 'Kirtans' 'Panchali' and 'Brata-Katha' are very common in religious functions. But the Manipuri literature did not remain neglected. 'Samjok Ngamba', 'Takhel Ngamba' 'Ouwa Ngamba' 'Khaki Ngamba' etc. are the accounts of some military exploits written in Manipuri during this period, 'Chothe Thangwai Pakhangba' and 'Sanamanik' are the two notable romantic tales. 'Chingthang Khomba Gangachatpa' is an account of Maharaja Bhagyachandra's pilgrimage to Nabadwip. Besides these, several stories from the Ramayana and the Mahabharata had been rewritten or translated in Manipuri. Angou Gopai translated the *Rnmayana* of Krittibash and the *Mahabharata* of Kashiramdas. It should be borne in mind that for more than twenty-five years following the death of Maharaja Bhagyachandra life in Manipur was violently disturbed by struggles for succession, civil war and successive Burmese invasions. Destructions caused by the Burmese invasions were so thorough that even after the conclusion of the Burmese War it took a long time for the restoration of normal life and the return of stability in Manipur. Obviously this period was devoid of the congenial atmosphere necessary for literary pursuits.

On the whole the medieval period in Manipuri literature proved to be a period of assimilation of new ideas, the effect of which was prominently manifested in the social and religious planes. Starting with the ideal of Gaudya Vaishnavism the native genius of Manipur evolved a new social norm and decorum of high aesthetic merit which are still being observed with utmost precision and almost universally. Indeed, Gaudya Vaishnavism has been virtually transformed into Manipuri Vaishnavism.

Manipuri literature entered into the modern age nearly in the beginning of the twentieth century. The literary talent is now expressing itself in various fields, i.e., in those of lyric, novel, drama, short story, history, grammar, astronomy, religion etc.

Although the modern form of language is traceable in some early works like 'Chandrakirti Jila Changba' written in the nineteenth century, real literary merit flourished for the first time in the works of Chaoba and Kamal.

Chaoba (1895-1950) was basically a poet. He commenced his literary career by composing melodious lyrics. In his compositions he suitably adopted the form of old ballads. Many of his poems bear the mark of a deep under-current of the philosophic query about the transitoriness of life. His essays though didactic in nature are still regarded as models of form as well as content.

The most favourite writer of the common man is Kamal (Dr. Kamal Singh), a contemporary of Chaoba. His 'Madhavi" (novel) won for him a place of love and esteem in every Manipuri heart. He was also a poet of merit. Words would come to him smoothly. A feeling of disappointment due to the imperfections of life and yearning for the perfection are the two underlying notes of his poems which have distinguished him as an idealist. His premature death has deprived the Manipuri literature of many more gems from him.

Hijam Angahal Singh is another stalwart in the field of modern Manipuri literature. He almost opened up a new horizon by compiling the scattered fragments of the epic poem 'Khamba Thoibi Sheireng' in blank verse of fourteen syllables. His 'Shingen Indu' is a narrative poem of love. He was equally adept in prose. As a novelist he showed his maturity in 'Jahera' which is a story of love between a Hindu young man and a Muslim girl. Dorendrajit Singh made his mark in 'Kangsha Badh'. A. Shyamsundar Singh translated Bankim Chandra's 'Kapal Kundala'. 'Abhijnana Shakuntalam' was translated by Vasudev Sharma. But the most successful among those translators is H. Nabadwip Chandra. By combining his poetic genius with his knowledge of Bengali language he placed before the readers the Manipuri version of Maichael Madhushudan Dutta's 'Meghnad Badh Kavya' without impairing in any way the force of language and the richness of imagination found in the original version. This went a long way in ensuring confidence in the capacity of the Manipuri language in expressing complex moods, lofty imaginations and rich thoughts. Thus in the early part of the modern period Manipuri literature was served by a band of literary giants who dedicated themselves solely to it.

After the Second World War literary consciousness gathered momentum and it has now turned nearly into a mass-movement. Pen is no longer the monopoly of the few. Even many among teen-agers are endeavouring to express themselves in writing. Yet there are some in this field who have proved their competence in guiding this movement. In the field of poetry A. Minaketan Singh with his new experiments is a bridge between the old (i.e. pre-war period) and the new (post-war period). But his fame is more established in literary criticism where he is a pioneer. His prose combines both grace and charm. 'Chatlasinei Kadaidano Ibani" of E. Nilakanta is a typical example of the direction in which Manipuri poetry is moving. Departing from the traditional theme, form, imagery and diction he has cast his poems into the mould of modern poetry. With him Manipuri poetry is not confined only to the rhythmic expressions of inspired feelings. It many also just convey the experience of complex sensibilities. In 'Tollaba sha Adugi Wakhal' N. Biren has placed modern poetry on firm footing. Iboposhak Singh also has made his mark in modern free verse. But the most celebrated poet of this age is L. Somorendra. Poetry with him is not a conscious effort. It flows spontaneously from his soul. Sincerity in expressions as in 'Wa Amatta Haige Telanga' and mobility in style might favour his poems with a lasting place. He is also experimenting with gentle satires. 'Ithak Ipom' of Nilabir is an expression of idealism. Besides those R. K. Madhubir, R. K. Surendra and E. Rajanikanta and many others are enriching in their own way the treasure of Manipuri poetry. T. Thoibi Devi B. Jayanta Kumar Sharma and Kh. Prakash have established their reputation in composing modern songs.

In the post-war period Manipuri literature is marching ahead in the field of novels also. 'Ima' and 'Rohini" of R.K.

Shitaljit are widely read. T. Thoibi Devi with her feminine touch has successfully revealed the gentler aspects of life in 'Radha', 'Nugshi Ichel', 'Chingda Shatpi Ingellei'. 'Na Tathiba Ahal Ama,' 'Hajj' and 'Hayad Begum' of Pacha Mitei have already attracted the attention of the readers. But 'Khudol' has earned a rare distinction for H. Guno Singh by receiving Jamini Sundar Gold Medal of the Manipur Sahitya Parishad. His 'Laman' and 'Aroiba Paodam' are also quite absorbing. Various experiences of life are reflected in his works. 'Eidi Oktabini" of Kh. Ibohal is an erotic novel. The central theme in most of the novels is a love story.

With the rapid growth in the number of journals and magazines there has been nearly a boom in the cutput of short stories. Along with many others Prakash, Nilabir, Biren, Chitreshwar, Dinamani, Tejamani, M. K. Binodini are also there. M. K. Binodini is a talented writer. She combines judgement with refineness in projecting her new ideas.

Besides those creative poets, novelists and story writers there are others who have enriched Manipuri literature by translating selected works from Sanskrit, Bengali, Hindi and English literatures. Late Panditraj Atombapu Sharma translated 'Chanakya Niti" the 'Chaitanya Charitamrita', the 'Gita', the 'Atharba Veda' and many other Sanskrit works. He has also to his credit some original works of both religious and secular nature. A. Braja Bihari Sharma has translated some of the works of Kalidas. Kalachand Shastri is distinguished for his translation of the 'Mahabharata'. His other important works are History of Manipuri literature, 'Ashamba Manipuri Sahityagi Itihas' and 'Manipuri Vaykaran Kaumudi'. He has been awarded 'Padmashri' by the President of India. But Pandit Achouba M. Chandra Singh is one of those few learned scholars who are holding the key to the gateway of ancient Manipuri wisdom. For seeking veracity of any information or interpretation of any script or validity of any opinion he is often referred to. Exploring in the field of ancient Manipuri literature, N. Khelachandra Singh has brought out 'Manipuri Shahityagi Ariba Itihash'. Prof. Nandalal Sharma's special field of study is Manipuri philology. Manipuri Sahitya Parishad has translated some old Manipuri texts into modern Manipuri. It will not be out of place to mention that H. Irabot Singh, the prominent revolutionary leader of Manipur in the early post-war period, was a promising writer and is one of the founder members of the Manipuri Sahitya Parishad.

Along with the different branches works on literary criticism and technique are also coming up. 'Meitei Upanyash' of A. Minaketan, 'Achaiba Lei" and 'Manipuri Kavitagi Chhanda' of E Nilakanta, 'Shahitya Neinaba wareng' of A.C. Singh, 'Chhanda veena' of R. K. Surendra, 'Manipuri Shahitya Amasung Shahityakar' of E. Dinamani Singh and 'Liklam' of Ch. Manihar Singh are informative and thought provoking. These are serving as guides to both the readers and writers. H. Gouradas Singh is also busy in enriching this branch of Manipuri literature.

6

Culture

R. K. Jhalajit Singh

MANIPUR is a land of music, dance and drama. The artistic urge is strong. But unlike most other places in India, there has not been much scope to satisfy the urge in fine architecture and somehow painting too did not reach great heights until the early years of British paramountcy. In the region, the people express themselves mostly through music, dance and drama.

Music of the valley may be divided into folk music and classical music. In the former category are included the types of songs known as *khullang ishei*, *lai haraoba ishei*, *pena ishei* and *Khongjong parva*. *Ishei* in Manipuri means music.

Khullang ishei is folk song *par excellence*. No one engages a teacher to learn it. One hears it sung in the village, in the vast rice-fields, the spacious slopes of the hills or on the silent waters of Logtag lake and one learns it instinctively. The theme in almost all cases is love. This type of song is seldom heard in the town unless it is in the theatre. There is a fixed set of tunes but the wording may be varied almost without limit to suit the mood and taste of the singer or singers and the wording is just fitted in the tunes.

Lai haraoba ishei is a type of song sung in a class of ceremonies called *lai haraoba.* These songs are full of erotic mysticism but the real meaning is veiled by the use of innocent sounding words. They are accompanied with dances.

Pena ishei or simply *pena* is a class of songs sung to the accompaniment of a stringed musical instrument also called *pena.* A small piece of slender bamboo is fastened to the shell of a dry gourd, or a coconut. A tuft of hair of horse-tail is fastened to the bamboo and the shell. Another tuft of horse-tail is fastened to a curved iron rod. Some tiny bells also are fastened to the curved iron rod to give a jingling sound. The bamboo is held in the left hand and the shell is slightly pressed against the chest and the curved iron rod is held in the right hand. The tuft on the bamboo is rubbed with that on the curved iron rod and sound is produced. The tension of the tuft on the bamboo is controlled by the fingers of the left hand.

The theme of this class of music is in most cases the story of the lovers, Khamba and Thoibi. In rare cases, it is some legend or some charm to ensure the prosperity of the village.

The singer of *pena* is clad in a snow-white *dhoti* and puts on a turban of the same colour. He puts on gold bangles and gold earrings. He is clean in his person and his dress, and sometimes, puts on flowers. He is assisted by one or two young learners, usually his pupils.

Formerly, *pena* had a more varied use such as waking up the king early in the morning or following him in his tours behind his elephant.

A new type of songs resembling folk music is *Khongjong parva.* Khongjong is a place some 35 kilometers to the south of Imphal. It was the theatre of the most decisive and sanguinary battle in the fight against the British in the War of 1891. It is sung solo accompanied by a *dholak* only. The word *parva* occurring in *Khongjong parva* means a definite part of an epic like *Bhishma parva, Drona parva,* etc. Soon after the battle of Khongjong in which the Manipuris were defeated, a type of songs to commemorate the heroic struggle of the Manipuris came into existence. Since the last and the most decisive, and therefore the most important, battle was fought at Khongjong, the type of music is called *Khongjong parva.*

Soon other themes were set to the tune of *Khongjong parva.* Historical themes, such as Jai Singh's flight to the court of King Rajeshwar of Assam and Chandrakriti's meeting with Lord Northbrook, the Governor-General of India, in 1874 became popular. Episodes from the *Ramayana* and the *Mahabharta* too were set to its tune and became popular in their new garb also. The story of Khamba and Thoibi and some other old love stories also are now sung in the form of *Khongjong parva.*

An almost extinct type of folk music is *thabal chongba.* This was the type of music which used to accompany the form of dance of the same name. It was tuneful and was sung by a large group of young men and women dancing in a ring in the moonlight. The theme was either religious or historical.

The most important classical music of Manipur is *nat.* It is used in all ceremonies such as the piercing of the ears, the investiture of the sacred thread, marriage, *shardha*, etc., and festivals like Jhulon and Durga Puja. Manipuri *ras* is invariably preceded by *nat* songs.

The star singer is assisted by a team including two drummers. He puts Vaishnava sect marks on his face and eleven other places on his body. He is clad in a *dhoti*, puts on a turban on his head and a sheet of cloth is tied round his waist. Snow-white is the colour of his dress. He uses a pair of cymbals called *kartal* fitted with purple or yellow straps. His songs are sometimes accompanied with some simple dances. Hence the name *nat* song. *Nata* in Sanskrit means a dancer or an actor.

The star singer is assisted by a team including two drummers. The entire team including the star singer and the drummers is called one *pala.* There is good team work in a *pala*; a few sing while he sings to swell the volume of the song and others sing after he stops. The leader of the latter group is called *duhar*. The drummers, dressed like the rest of the team except that their turbans are smaller, get one or two chances to impress the audience with their skill in percussion and their spectacular virile drum dance.

In *nat*, the music is begun with one of the six *ragas.* It is compulsory and cannot be skipped. A *raga* is a series of musical tones rigidly fixed in a particular order. Each *raga*, if correctly rendered, is believed to produce its own effect. Correct rendering of Shri Raga, for instance, is believed to confer prosperity and is therefore suitable for ceremonies like marriage. Selection of a suitable *raga* for the occasion calls for good taste and maturity of judgment. It is the prerogative of the star singer. Rendering of a *raga* in *nat* singing, specially the principal *raga,* is a most solemn thing. Any act of omission or commission will, it is believed, produce bad effects on the star singer, and the householder or the persons for whom the ceremony is held.

The *raga* finished, next stage is to sing the glory of Chaitanya, to whose school of Vaishnavism the Manipuri Hindus belong. There are a large number of songs dedicated to his glory or activities and are called *Gour pads.* The word *Gour* in *Gour pads* is an abbreviation of Gouranga, another name of Chaitanya and *pads* is colloquialism for *pada*, a line or lines in a poem or song.

After the *Gour pads*, they sing the glory of Krishna and his exploits in Vrindavan. Last of all comes the prayer in which nothing, not even heaven is prayed for except the desire to serve His feet in tens of millions of re-births.

Gulabi Singh, Ibomacha Sharma (better known as Abhiram) and Kalidoman Singh are among the leading *nat* singers at present.

Not included in classical music but partaking of their nature are two types of songs called *dhob* and *manohar sai. Dhob* is sung with a kind of large but thin cymbals called *jhal.* It is accompanied with the beating of drums in the Manipuri style.

The singers use turbans but they are smaller than those used by *nat* singers. Upto the Thirties of this century, *dhob* singers wore a kind of shirt called *bagal bandhi* which was not unlike the shirts worn by Muslim rulers. But they were very thin and spotlessly white. The shirt of the star singer was long and flowing and reached upto the shin, but in other respects it was like the shirts of other members of his team. Nowadays such shirts are seldom seen.

A very common theme of *dhob* songs is how Sanatan, a minister of Hussain Shah, escaped from his prison and became Chaitanya's disciple. It may be mentioned that two Brahmin brothers assuming Muhammadan names served under Hussain Shah as his ministers. Afterwards they came to be known as Rup and Sanatan. Rup resigned and became Chaitanya's disciple. Suspecting that Sanatan would follow suit, Hussain Shah put him into the prison. Sanatan escaped from there and became a great disciple of Chaitanya. *Dhob* singers describe how he escaped and where and how he met Chaitanya.

In tune, *dhob* songs are intermediate between *nat* songs and *manohar sai*, which is described below.

Manohar sai tunes originated in the Manohar Sai *pargana* in the district of Burdwan in Bengal. Hence the name. As in other fields the Vaishnavaites rejected time-honoured conventions in the field of music also. *Manohar Sai* tune sounds like a cry from the innermost recesses of the devotee's heart in his yearning for God, and bring tears to the eyes of the hearers by appealing to his finer sentiments. As in *nat*, very often the whole assembly—singers, drummers, conch-blowers and hearers—shed happy tears together and the place, wherever it may be, becomes for the time being one of the holiest of the holy places.

Manohar sai reached Manipur in the 19th century. It is sung with a kind of small cymbals called *ram kartal* and a couple of drums called *khol*. The *manohar sai* singer does not use any turban and his team is smaller than that of the *nat* singer.

During the festivals of Rath Yatra, Jhulan and Durga Puja, we find teams of women singers. Among types of songs sung by women, we may mention *nupi pala*, *nupi khubaishei*, *ras* and *rasheshwari*. In the first two varieties, little girls may have their own teams but the last two are sung only by adults. The last mentioned is a variety of *nat* adopted to suit women singers.

Nupi pala literally means a women's team of singers. But the drummers are men. In *nat*, the songs are invariably begun with a *raga* as we have seen, but in the case of *nupi pala*, they are begun with a series of tones softer and less elaborate than those of a *raga*.

A *nupi pala* singer devotes much time to her hair-dressing and, if she is a married woman, occasionally uses flowers for her chignon. There is no special costume for the *nupi pala* singer. She holds a pair of little cymbals called *mandira* fitted with crimson straps. A chaperon accompanies her at night. It is sung during Jhulan and Durga Puja.

In *khubaishei*, no cymbal is used. Time is kept by clapping hands. In Manipuri, *khubak* means palm and *ishei* means music. *Khubaishei* is a combination of *khubak* and *ishei* and therefore literally means palm music or music sung to the accompaniment of the clapping of hands. It is sung either by men or women but not jointly. If it is sung by a team of men, it is called *nupa khubaishei* or men's *khubaishei*. It is sung in a vigorous *tandav* style and has an appeal of its own. If *khubaishei* is sung by a team of women, it is called *nupi khubaishei*. *Nupi* means women.

The dress in *nupi khubaishei* is like that of *nupi pala*. But *khubaishei* is almost wholly sung standing, unlike *nupi pala*, which is sung sitting. The theme is Krishna's going from Vrindavan to Mathura to kill the demoniac king Kansa and the sorrow of milkmaids. It may be remarked that in the story narrated in the Tenth Book of the *Bhagavat* Krishna was accompanied by his elder brother Balarama and his foster-father Nanda, and the sorrowing milkmaids never went near him but unobtrusively watched the sad departure from a distance. In the songs sung in *khubaishei*, the presence of Balarama and Nanda is entirely deleted and thus the milkmaids can freely come near Krishna. The songs depict them as sobbing and weeping and physically obstructing his chariot by seizing the wheels with their hands and tying their hair to them.

Khubaishei is sung during the Rath Yatra festival.

Songs accompanying dances in the performance of Krishna's *raslila* form a class by themselves. They are deeply religious specially those sung in *Maha ras.*

Dances of the valley may also be discussed under two heads : folk and classical. In the folk group, we include *thabal chongba* and *lai haraoba.* In the classical group we include *ras* dances.

Thabal chongba is or rather was a beautiful form of dance. The name means dancing in the moonlight. It was held at night of the fullmoon of Lamda and during the next five days. The spacious courtyards of nobles and rich men or the village greens were the ideal places for this dance. Young boys and girls, clean in person and clean in clothes, danced in a ring in the moonlight singing sweet songs. There was a boy between every two girls. The dance was neither intricate nor very laborious. Every young girl and every boy knew how to dance and they were expected to join it unless there was some special reason such as illness in the family or the death of a near relative.

Nowadays the practice of restricting the dance to six days is completely broken. The dance continues far into the dark fortnight and sometimes even beyond. The place of the moonlight is taken by fluorescent lights in the town and by gas lanterns in the village. The dance movements have been much simplified.

Lai haraoba dances form a group of graceful movements performed to please the gods. The dances are accompanied with songs which are called *lai haraoba* songs. The more important of the instruments are *pena* and drums.

Manipuri *ras* is a dance-drama, not merely a dance, on the theme of Krishna's play with the milkmaids of Vrindavan. There are four kinds of Manipuri *ras* viz. *Vasanta ras*, *Kunja ras*, *Maha ras* and *Nata ras.*

Vasanta ras is played in the spring on the fullmoon of

Sajibu (about April). On this night, the dance is performed at the temple of Govindajee and after it, it may be performed anywhere else. The plot is mainly based on the beautiful Sanskrit lyric *Geet Govinda* of Jaya Deva. *Kunja ras* is played in autumn on the fullmoon of Mera (about October). It is short and is based on the *Bhagavat*.

The most important of the *rasas* is *Maha ras*, as the name implies. It is based on five chapters called *Ras Panchadhyai* in the Tenth Book of the *Bhagavat*. The five chapters are considered the holiest part of the holy book. Apart from the religious aspect, *Maha ras* is a really beautiful dance-drama from the stand point of art. The glittering costumes of the milkmaids and Krishna in a pleasing colour combination look very beautiful in the artificial light in the *mandap* or on the stage. The tuneful accompanying music narrates the story. The movements of the fingers and hands speak a language of their own specially to those who know the meaning of these signs. To those who do not, they are graceful parts of the show. It is performed in late autumn.

Maha ras was considered to be too sacred for show before audiences of non-Vaishnavas or for presentation on the stage. It was not until about 1970 that a stage version of *Maha ras* began to appear. But British Political Agents of the 19th century sometimes expressed their desire to the Maharaja to see Manipuri *ras*. To fulfil their wishes, which it was not expedient to brush aside lightly, but without offending the susceptibility of an orthodox society, a new *ras* was composed. The result was *Nata ras*.

Nata ras is not based on any specific scripture. The plot differs materially from that given in the *Bhagavat*, or *Geet Govinda*. The head dress of the milkmaids is different and the songs are suitably modified. But the styles of the dance are the same. *Nata ras* may be played at any time of the year ; there is no restriction. But it is not played at the temple of Govindajee.

Shri Leichonbam Koirang Singh, a recipient of Natya Akademi award, has recently discovered *Ras Pareng*, a complete set of graceful modes of beating the drum expressing the entire *ras*.

There is a popular dance-opera called *sanjenba* which literally means tending the cattle. It is about Krishna's tending cattle in the groves of Vrindavan and is based on the Tenth Book of the *Bhagavat*, with slight alterations here and there. It is essentially a dance-opera of young boys. Young girls also, if dressed as boys, may take part in it. We call it a dance-opera because it is a fine drama in which the parts are sung to the accompaniment of dances and acting. We find it existing in the reign of Madhu Chandra (1800-1806).

Drama began in this part of India on religious themes. Vaishnavism being the court-religion, some of the dramas were organised by the Government. This was the practice upto 1891.

But the theatre, by which we mean a permanent house with a stage and in which dramatic performances are regularly held, is a gift of the British period. Soon after the upheavals of 1891, Bengali officers and teachers settled in the State. They were fond of drama and staged amateur plays in a theatre in their official colony. This caught the imagination of the student community. Within a few years, students organised plays and staged them during Saraswati Puja. These early plays were in Bengali. The young Maharaja, Sir Chura Chand Singh, was a patron of fine arts and sports. Under his aegis, a number of plays were produced in Manipuri and were staged at the palace.

The first regular society of amateur actors was formed about the year 1931 under the name M.D.U. A costly outhouse was turned into a theatre at the residence of Shri Shyam Kishore Singh, a judicial officer of the State and a brother of the Maharani, and the M.D.U. began to stage social and historical plays. After a chequered career, the society built its permanent theatre at its present site in Police Lines, where it is still staging plays regularly.

The war years from 1942 to 1946 saw a boom of dramas. Theatres grew up like mushrooms. But the same years saw the increasing popularity of the films also. In the tussle between the theatre and the cinema, the latter won and theatres withered away. Only about three or four theatres remained in the field.

Most of the plays are original writings and some are translations from Bengali and Sanskrit. Among the latter, we may mention M.D.U.'s *Shakuntala,* a translation from the immortal Kalidasa's drama of the same name. The translation is happy, the acting convincing and the scenery and the light effect are fine.

Among famous playwrights we may mention G.C. Tongbra, Ramacharan and Biramangol. There is an institution sponsored by the Government under the name of Manipur State Kala Akademi to look after the improvement of the fine arts particularly, music, dance, drama and literature.

Until about the first air-raid of Imphal by the Japanese in May 1942, Manipur was a land of operas. There were professional opera parties consisting mainly of sweet-voiced girls. In the dry months from about the end of the harvest to about the beginning of rains, they used to roam throughout the valley providing inexpensive but wholesome entertainment. The themes were always religious. During the war years, the cinema flourished and the cinema is a serious competitor not only of the drama but also of the opera. In the fierce competition, the opera languished for want of customers.

But there is an opera which is still existing. It is the *Gour Lila* based on episodes from the life of Chaitanya and his companion, Nityananda.

Vaishnavism struck roots in Bengal, as in many other places in the country, long before the birth of Chaitanya. But it was he who gave it a wonderful renaissance. *Gour Lila* is based on the episodes in Chaitanya's life, but with some deviation. The most striking deviation is the deification of Chaitanya. During his lifetime, Chaitanya emphatically denied that he was an incarnation of God. Tendency of deification being very strong in India, he was nonetheless deified soon after his death.

A word is necessary about the emotion of the participants.

Very often the situation demands that the actor or the actress should weep. When that happens, participants weep naturally shedding natural tears. The whole opera is performed in a religious atmosphere and most participants join it not for money or even fame but as an act of piety. That is the reason of their natural sobbing and weeping at appropriate moments.

There is a class of plays called *Shumang Lila.* These are dramatic performances with proper acting make-up and costume but presented in the open air without stage, scenery or light effect. The courtyard is the usual place where it is performed. Hence the name *Shumang Lila—Shumang* means courtyard.

In the open courtyard, spectators sit on all sides leaving some vacant place at the centre. This roughly serves the purpose of the stage. A little from it, there is a place, often in the verandah or an out-house, temporarily screened off. It is the 'green room'. Women's roles are played almost invaribly by young men. With skilful make-up, art and acting, the young men are more woman-like than real women and prettier too, although temporarily. When an actor finishes his part, he retires to the 'green room' or may sit on a mat in the open space mentioned above.

Since there is no stage, there is no curtain and the play is not divided into acts or scenes as in the theatre. But acts and scenes are there and spectators divide them in their own minds. There is no scenery to help the spectator know where the dialogue is taking place—whether in a town, the village common or in the wood. The deficiency must be made up by the imagination of the spectator with the help of the dialogue, which often suggests the locale in the first one or two sentences. There is no special light arrangement to suggest night, dusk or dawn. Again, the actors must depend on the fertile imagination of the spectators. But in spite of these drawbacks the *Shumang Lila* is popular.

The plays are mostly social plays nowadays. Formerly they were traditional plays. *Harishchandra, Moirang Parva Chandra-*

has, *Chandrajini* and *Thog Lila* were some of the most successful *Shumang Lilas*. A word is necessary about *Chandrajini* The play is based on the story of *Chandrajini* found only in the Manipuri version of the Lanka Canto of the *Ramayana*. It is a skilful interpolation by Manipuri *warilibas* or professional story tellers. *Thog Lila* was a type by itself. *Thog* means a professional swindler and the story began with the exploits of a cheat. But on the whole, it was a conglomeration of political sermons, singing verses exposing man's foibles, such as his weakness, even at an advanced age, for beautiful wives. Humour was the stock-in-trade of the actors in *Thog Lila* and they were rewarded with peals of laughter from the spectators.

Shumang Lila is not very expensive. A well-to-do person invites a troupe and the play is performed in his courtyard and men, women and children of the locality witness it free.

People of the hill areas of the State are interested in song and dance. The Kabuis have some developed dances accompanied with songs. These are performed during their annual festivals. In winter, usually in December or January, they have an annual festival and they sing and dance far into the night. They have also some folk songs. One such song is about the contemplated departure of a marriageable girl after her marriage to the house of the bridegroom in the far off village covered with mists. The Tangkhuls too have some sweet folk songs. People of the south-western hills of Manipur have a kind of dance in which the dancers jump over pieces of bamboo. The Kabuis have produced a few dramas in their mother-tongue.

7

Daring Dames of Manipur

R. K. Murthi

WOMEN, all over the world, are clamouring for equal rights. The militancy shown by some women in the developed nations to focus attention on the inequity which still prevails in the relation between man and woman, giving man all the advantages, has been much more marked during the last decade. Women have protested by buring bras, by dumping children on the laps of their husbands while at work in their offices, demanded that men should share the domestic chores, insisted that they would remould society so that all differences would be wiped out. All differences except the one that comes with nature, the difference which remains a matter of gender.

The militancy of the women of the West is a modern phenomenon. Not so the spirit of defiance which runs through the women of Manipur. Of course, it would be running against reality to claim that perfect equality between man and woman has been in existence in Manipur. But there is certainly no excessive male dominance which puts women out of reckoning. Instead, what we find in Manipur is a liberal approach to the entire gamut of man-woman relationship. Women do not carry a grudge against the men for being dominant or aggressive. They have the sense of being almost equal to men in many respects. This sense of equality springs from the prime role women play in bringing an additional income to the family. Many of the women spend their spare time weaving baskets. They produce, out of cane, exotic designs. The myriad shapes and sizes which go with the baskets are eye-catching. The women are not content with producing the baskets. They take them out, to the market, sell them, either wholesale to one or other of the major outlets, or they sit with their pile of baskets, spread out before them, ready to wrangle over the price with any customer. The women haggle over the price, gently, but firmly, negotiate the final price, give the customer a gentle smile as he moves off.

It is a usual sight to see women, carrying heavy loads of vegetables to the market. There is an exclusive market managed entirely by women. They carry on their business with perfect confidence and competence. They present the picture of women who know that they too are bread winners, that they don't have to fight, like their counterparts in the so-called developed nations, for liberation.

It is economic freedom which gives the women of Manipur their status. They don't shy away from any chores. They work, along with the men, whether it be in the fields, removing weeds and pests, ploughing the fields, sowing and reaping the harvest, beating the rice stalks to get the paddy and the chaff separated, carrying the paddy to dry, pounding the paddy to get the rice out of the husk.

There is no task which is considered soft or unwomanly. One of the sights which a visitor to Manipur will never forget, all his life, is the array of women, standing in knee-deep water in one lake or the other, their nets spread out for fish. They stand, like statues, letting the sun tipple over their nose-rings or ear rings, dazzle into colours which give grace to the rainbow. The light sheens through the ornaments, dips down to paint colourful versions on the surface of the lakes too. A writer who visited the State told me that the women, standing out in the shallow waters, made him think of lotuses in full bloom. Coming from Kerala in the South, he added that the scenerio reminded him of the backwaters of Kerala. The comparison was not odious. For in Kerala, too, women have enjoyed, all through history, a fair amount of equal rights. In fact there was a time when matrilineal system was potent and the centre of the family was the woman and not the man.

It is economic liberty which gives the women of Manipur their liberation from old world concepts.

This is not something new to the land.

According to tradition. when the first king Chitrasen died, he left a daughter, Princess Chitrangada. None of the citizens questioned the right of the princess to ascend the throne. On the other hand, they agreed that the throne was hers by right. This reflects the liberal attitude of the people towards the fair sex.

Naturally, the women of Manipur are more aggressive. They refuse to stay back when any measure or step by the regime threatens to make a serious impact on their economic well-being. When the occasion demands, they plunge into the thick of the struggle. And more often than not, they have proved that women power has enough teeth to bring the stiffest opposition down on its knees.

A few instances, culled from the history of Manipur, will sustain this tenet.

In 1904, the house of the British Assistant Political agent in Imphal was burnt down by some miscreants. This was considered a major threat to the authority of the regime by the British Resident Maxwell. He decided to come down with a heavy hand, to drive home the point that none could dare to take on the Britishers. He ordered that the local populace should contribute the labour and the material to raise a new structure at the spot where the old building once stood. The order struck the women as unjust. Should not Maxwell pin down the crime on those who were responsible, make them pay for their crime ? Why should they pay for the inefficiency of the regime to track down the criminals? This plea was put forth by them forcibly. Even today, the role of women in this episode is narrated with excitement and pride by all Manipuris.

They refer to this as one of the several battles fought by the women. They call it a Nupi (Women) Lan (War).

Nearly twenty-five years later, the women proved their might again.

The regime imposed a new tax which threatened to make inroads into the economy of the people. The women organised protest marches. They shouted slogans, demanding the repeal of the new impost. Finally, an Englishman who was the President of the Durbar came to assess the situation. The women pleaded with him. When he refused to see their viewpoint, they bundled him and dipped him in the lake. They let him go, but the message was clear.

Later came Stewart, another Englishman. He came to settle the dispute about fishing rights in the Loktak Lake. He set out in a boat with some leaders of the area, hoping to listen to their complaints. The news that Stewart had come spread like wild fire. Women gathered in large numbers. They formed a big cordon round the boat jetty. They raised slogans, starting that no power on earth could curb their rights to fish in the lakes. The din and noise raised by the women reached Stewart and his party. Stewart stared, with open mouth at the large crowd of women. One of the local leaders on board the boat warned him that the dames were out to get their pound of flesh. Stewart had never faced such a dangerous situation. He sensed that the women would pounce on him, tear him to pieces if he did not yield to their demands. Of course he was wise enough also to realise that the women would not have been so militant but for the fact that the proposed move by the regime would leave them economically poorer.

The official asked the boatmen to row back to the jetty. The shouts and screams of the women gained in crescendo as the boat moved towards the shore. Stewart told one of the local leaders to announce to the women that the President of the Durbar had conceded their demand. Those words fell like sweet music on their ears. They cheered Stewart, hailed him for the wise decision. It was a battle, won by them, without raising any weapon. The only weapon was their voice power. Stewart had a taste of the power which lay in collective action. It was this victory which showed, once again, that the women of Manipur had the strength to fight for their rights.

Nine years later came the greatest test to the women power of Manipur.

Floods caused severe damage to standing paddy crops in the State. The price of paddy rose suddenly. The Maharaja examined the situation. He passed an order banning the export of rice from the State. The people welcomed this move.

But their happiness was short-lived.

Just when the harvesting was on, the order banning the export of rice was revoked. The people could not understand the justification for the move. A large group of women left their fields. They collected together and marched to the Durbar Hall. The Durbar was in session, even though the Maharaja Churachand Singh was away on a pilgrimage. The women raised slogans, cried out in strident notes, asking the officials to scrap the order and to reimpose a ban on the export of paddy.

Sharpe, the President of the Durbar, came out and met the agitators. He told them that he could do nothing as the order was issued by the Maharaja. Since the Maharaja was out of station, Sharpe said the people would have to wait for the return of the ruler.

This plea went unheeded.

The women assumed belligerent posture. They insisted that Sharpe should take immediate action. At last, Sharpe agreed to send a telegram to the Maharaja, conveying the demand of the women. The women shouted, "Well, do it, now."

Sharpe nodded his head. He came out, rode towards the telegraph office. The women gathered at the telegraph office. Sharpe came out, affirmed that he had already despatched the telegram. The women refused to let him go back to his residence. They insisted that he should wait at the telegraph office itself till the reply came. Sharpe stared at the women.

He tried to push his way through. But he found the cordon formed by the women impregnable.

The news that Sharpe had been kept captive by the women reached a British Major of the 4th Assam Rifles. He decided to go and find out. Along with him came the civil surgeon. The two were allowed by the women to move into the telegraph office. But when they tried to walk back, leading Sharpe too, they found the tight cordon of women all around. The civil surgeon tried to reason with the mob. The major tried to bamboozle them. But the women remained deaf to threats and platitudes. They were determined to get the ban reimposed. They were ready to face even bullets.

In the meanwhile, the news that their major was held hostage by a violent group of dames reached the men and officers of the Assam Rifles. They came rushing to the spot of trouble. The officer, leading the platoon, exhorted the people to disperse. But the appeal fell flat. None would listen to the plea. Instead, the women waved their arms, shouting, "Get the ban order imposed."

Someone said that it was time for Sharpe for his dinner. The dames replied, "We have had no food for over twelve hours. Can't Sharpe get his dinner delayed by an hour or two. We will let him go as soon as the offending order is withdrawn, as soon as the ban is reimposed."

The words roused the ire of the officer leading the men of the Assam Rifles. He told his men to get ready to disperse the mob. The women, noting the menacing stand of the armed men, picked up stones. The armed men ran into the crowd, their bayonets unsheathed. The women did not wince They stood their ground.

Unwilling to get embroiled in the impasse, the officer, leading the Assam Rifies cried halt to the assault. He removed a couple of women who were injured to the dispensary.

The icy wind of December did not deter the women. It was nearly midnight. Stars winked from above. The women pulled their shawls and their hoods closer to ward off the cold.

Time sped by. There was still no reply from the Maharaja. The women waited, confident that the Maharaja would finally repeal the new order.

Finally, at one a.m. the telegram came. It was the best piece of news which could have come to Sharpe. He came out, waving his hands, shouting that the ban on movement of rice outside the State has been reimposed. The women screamed in ecstasy. They danced, wildly, while the tired Sharpe, accompanied by the major and the civil surgeon, moved through the crowd and rode back to safety.

During the onslaught of Netaji's forces along with the Japanese army, many Manipuri women openly aligned themselves with the men of the INA. They gave succour to the freedom fighters, helped them to get food and supplies, led them through by-passes and little-known routes onward towards Kohima from where the INA hoped to come down to the plains of Assam.

What is the secret of this invincible courage of Manipuri women? Is it to be sought in the hoary tradition, set by Chitrangada? Is it to be traced to the clime of the land? Can it be attributed to the geographic location, with constant pressures from neighbouring nations, with incessant threats from nature, wild animals and natural risks?

Why should we bother about the forces which breathed courage and daring into the women? Enough to say that the women of Manipur are bold, almost defiant, and have an edge over the educated elite dames in the rest of the world. Manipur may not be a woman's world. But, it certainly is not a man's world either. It is here that one finds equality between the sexes achieved in a very harmonious setting.

8

Towards Prosperity

Shashi Ahluwalia

MANIPUR is making slow but steady progress towards prosperity.

Certain emerging trends in Manipur are indicative of better economic outlook for the state in the coming years, notwithstanding the uncertainty on the farm front owing to erratic rainfall. The commissioning of the Loktak hydel project is expected to ensure uninterrupted power.

A benevolent giant awoke to the service of the nation in Manipur in early May, 1983.

The Loktak hydro-electric project, with an installed capacity of 105MW and a generating 70,000 KW of power at 60 per cent load factor, has gone on stream, adding 48 million units of electricity annually to the country's power output.

Constructed at a cost of Rs. 113 crores, the Loktak is a multipurpose scheme, envisaged to produce power, to irrigate 23,000 hectares of land and to achieve flood control in the Loktak lake.

Located at Moisang, 39 km. south of Imphal, power from Loktak project will give a new impetus to the development of Assam, Nagaland, Mizoram and most of the North-Eastern States besides Manipur.

The project consists of 10.7 meter barrage at Ithai and a

trans-basin water conducting system 10.29 km. long, which includes an open channel section, a cut and cover section, a head race tunnel and penstocks. The surge shaft at the head of the penstock is 60 meter high and 9.15 meter in diameter. Three penstock pipes, each 2.286 in diameter brings the water down to the three 35MW generating units of the power station, built on the banks of the Leimatak river. Tail race waters are diverted into the Leimatak river through a channel.

Transmission lines to Imphal, Yerembam and Jiribam have already been drawn.

Work on the project began in 1971 under the direct charge of the Ministry of Irrigation and Power. Consequent to the organisation of the National Hydro-Electric Power Corporation (NHPC), the work was handed over to it on 1 January 1977. The comprehensive project report was drawn up by the Manipur Public Works Department in 1967.

In completing the Loktak project the NHPC can be justly proud. The project has many "firsts" in India to its credit. Its tunnel was the first in India to be completed under gassy conditions, methane gas filtering into it. An alpine Miner was used in India for the first time in Loktak. The unstable conditions of the area and the difficult terrain made the completion of the project a marvel of engineering.

The lives lost, the effort put in and the money and time invested have proved fruitful. However difficult the task has been, today, there is light, "at the end of the tunnel".

According to Dr. T.N. Saikia of Agro-Economic Research Centre, the problem of social and economic disparities amongst the people living in the hills and the plains, and to remove the regional imbalances both the Central and State Governments have undertaken special area development projects in the recent past.

The Nungba Project in West Manipur district, known as Integrated Hill Area Development Project (IHADP), was initiated in 1974-75. The project area lies in the western hill ranges of Manipur with a geographical area of 1295 sq. km. The elevation of the narrow valley ranges from about 350 m.

Manipur Tableaux moving down Rajpath, New Delhi during Republic Day Parade

The Chairman, Trade Fair Authority of India, presenting the First Award to the representative of Manipur Pavilion in 1981

A Manipuri woman busy at weaving

Manipuri craftswomen at work

ıeapple leaves crushing unit

Power tiller at work in Manipur

. Manipur crafts

A machine processing pineapple leaves

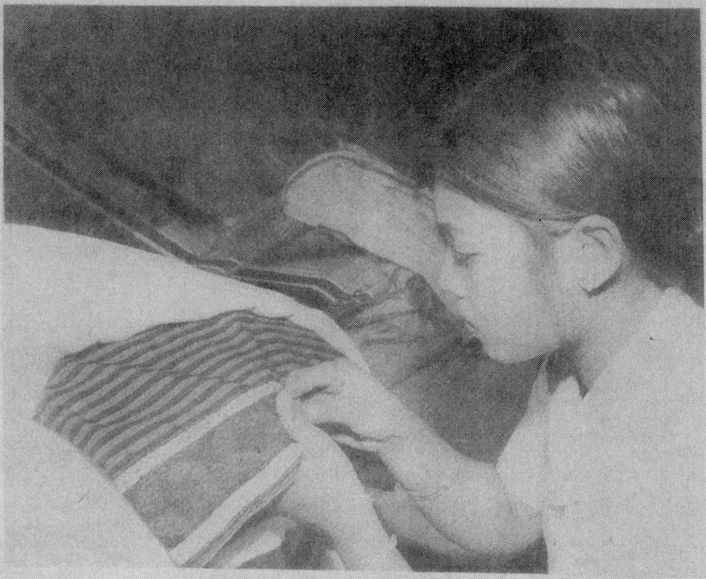

A Manipuri woman doing embroidery

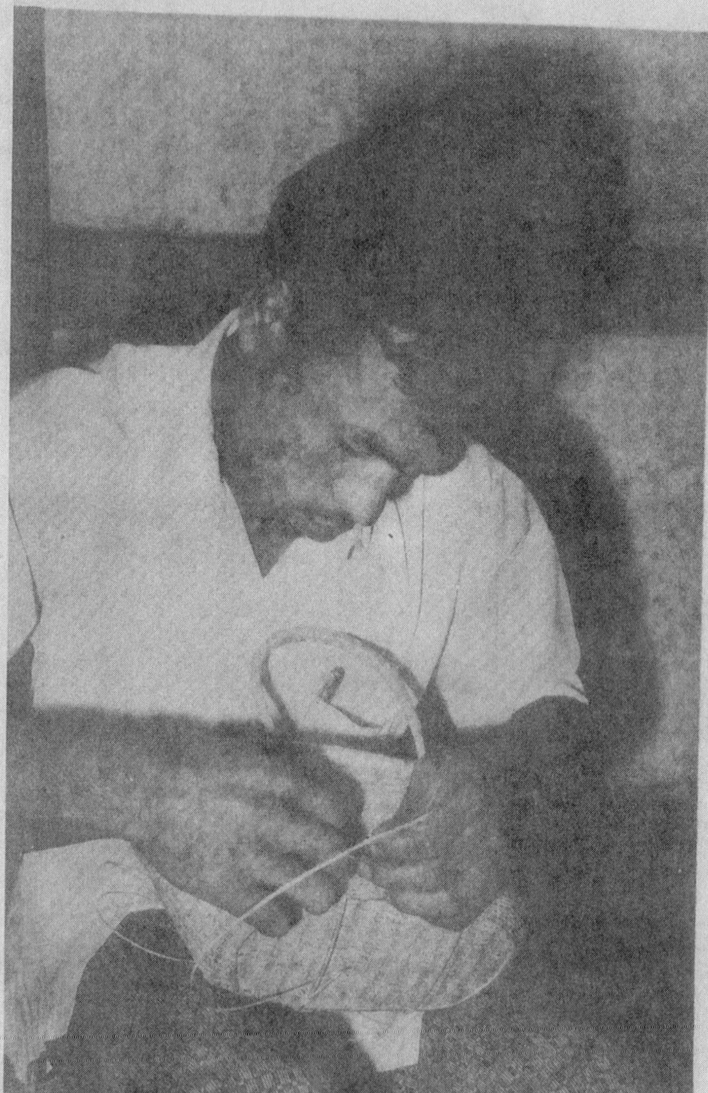

manipuri craftsmen making baskets

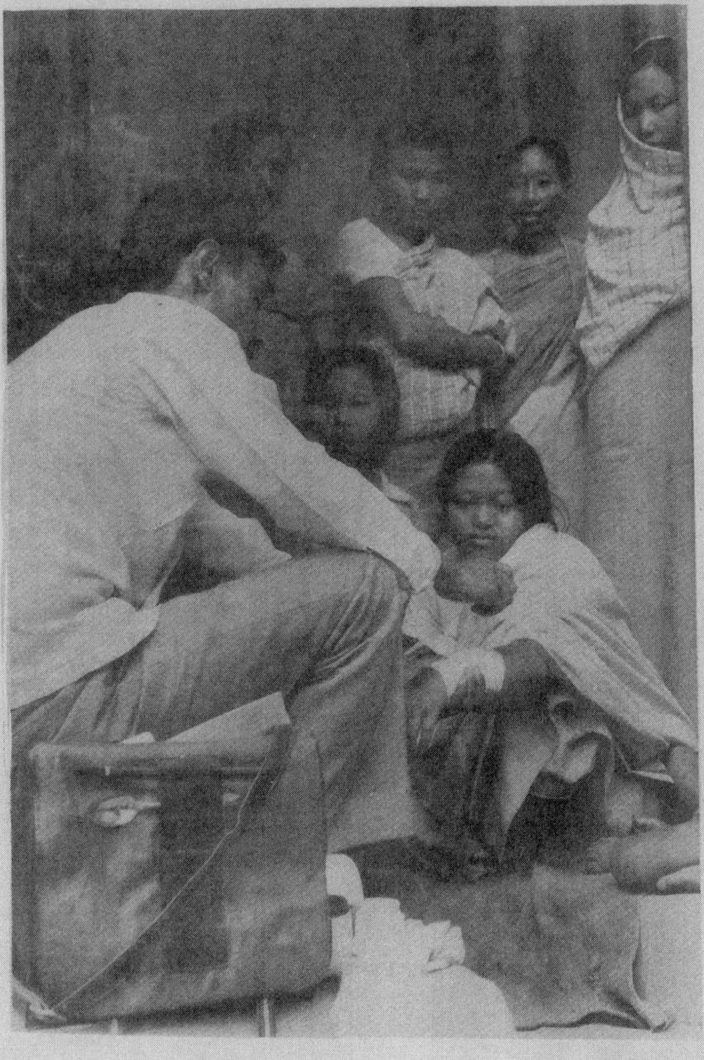

Community health worker in Manipur

Women casting vote
in Manipur

Site of Khoupum Dam

1.3 km. long penstock of
Loktak Hydro Power Project

Khoupum Dam in progress

Khoupum Dam inaugurated

to 800 m. and the hills within 800 m. to 2,000 m. above mean sea level. The main objectives of the IHAD project are :

(i) to help the hill farmers to take up integrated development schemes by way of diversifying the farming system through a phased programme of development ;

(ii) to wean away the Jhum cultivators from destructive farming practices and encourage settled farming ;

(iii) to introduce new technology in the field of agriculture and the allied sectors ;

(iv) to create basic infrastructure for rapid development of the project area.

The project was initiated with a Central assistance of Rs. 1.50 crores. The project had taken up agricultural development programmes with the introduction of HYV seeds, fertiliser plant protection measures, etc. together with double multiple cropping programme, development of horticulture by establishing progeny orchards for supply to the interested growers and rejuvenation of existing orchards ; land development by way of terracing and soil conservation ; creation of irrigation facilities by harnessing of small streams and rivulets by construction of dams, weirs and installation of pump sets for lift irrigation. Apart from these the project had also taken up the programme of introduction of improved dairy animals and poultry birds, creating marketing facilities, construction of link roads, facilities for cold storage, identification of growth centres, to link with interior areas.

The Agro-Economic Research Centre for North-East India at Jorhat evaluated the working of the project in 1978-79 (i.e. exactly after four years of functioning). Out of 58 main villages in the project area various project schemes were extended to 40 villages at the time of survey. Twelve villages, i.e., 30 per cent of the adopted villages were covered by the field level study in order to assess the effectiveness of the project programme at the field level. Attempt has also been made to focus the overall achievement of the project at the aggregate level.

The scheme-wise target for the project period and achievement during the four years of functioning were based on the data collected at the aggregate level. The overall achievement of the project in case of certain key schemes was not satisfactory.

In order to assess the impact of the overall project programmes the scheme-wise sample beneficiaries were interviewed. The project was chiefly aimed at boosting up of agricultural production with adoption of full package of practices including double/multiple cropping programme. Although the aggregate level study showed a spectacular progress in certain schemes, yet at the field level outcome was not very satisfactory. The HYV seeds covered a considerable area. The idea of introducing double/multiple cropping programme remains a theoretical proposition without any tangible results due to inadequate irrigation facility and the agricultural production process remains a gamble against monsoon. Other schemes like distribution of improved breeds of heifer, afforestation, rubber plantation, coffee plantation, etc. did not show any tangible achievements.

The key programme of introduction of bench type terraces with irrigation facility for settled farming in order to wean away the jhumias from destructive jhuming did not satisfy its objective. During the functioning of four years of the project only 22.65 per cent of the target was achieved and remaining 77 per cent left to be covered within another year. But of the total terraced land constructed under the project programme only about 31 per cent is irrigated and that too not perennially. The project planned to provide one hectare of irrigated terrace per family but the field study revealed that the project could provide only 1.33 acres per family on an average without adequate irrigation facility. The hill farmers took active interest in the project programme at the initial stage. But when the farmers found that yield of crops in few terraces even after introduction of HYV seeds, fertilisers and plant protection materials were not remunerative, they were disheartened about the introduction of modern inputs. This is perhaps due to soil. Humus was disturbed and not properly maintained at the time of preparation of terraces. So the hill farmers went back to jhuming to earn their livelihood.

In case of other schemes also the project could not make much headway except in the field of horticulture because of the fact that the agro-climatic condition is favourable to grow pineapple, orange, pear, etc. The horticultural schemes (particularly for pineapple) are facing marketing problems due to lack of proper communication and marketing facilities. The fruit canning and processing and marketing centres were not taken in hand as proposed. It was therefore feared that the horticulturists may not get fair return for their product. The presumption has amply been revealed by the fact that the oranges grown in the area are collected by the traders at throw away prices. The introduction of hybrid boar female piglets, cocks and cockerels may prove viable provided marketing and related infrastructural facilities are geared up.

The other schemes like afforestation, rubber plantation, citronella plantation as a measure to preserve valuable natural watersheds, were also taken up. These schemes were at initial stage of implementation at the time of field investigation and hence yet to show the viability.

From the review of development programmes of Nungba Project it may be said that the production oriented schemes achieved only partial success but ground work has been done by the Nungba Project to show the hill farmers the trend of development in the various fields.

The programme of changing the technology should be taken up stage by stage along with the distribution of inputs like HYV seeds, fertiliser plant protection materials through co-operatives to make the farmers involved in the process. Due to free distribution of inputs the people of the project area seem to have looked upon the project as benefit giver for all the time to come. The marketing of farm products would have also been arranged through the cooperatives in order to ensure fair price for their products, These aspects were not taken into account by the project for which the achievements are bound to be partial.

A section of farmers has taken to commercial farming. Investments in industrial ventures are picking up. The state has three growth areas : trade and commerce, road transport and the construction industry. Of these, the last is experiencing a veritable boom despite the fact that cement in this part of the country is priced quite high. There is room to believe that, given the present congenial industrial atmosphere and active government support, the state will soon be on the industrial map of India. One single factor that might largely contribute to the revival of economic activity is the commissioning of the Loktak hydro-electric project which is ensuring uninterrupted power supply.

There are unmistakable signs of entrepreneurship and investment picking up in this state. Greater intensive farming operations are giving rise to increasingly higher demand for water from the Loktak lift irrigation system. Significantly enough, the younger generation of farmers has been attracted to commercial farming. There is a great demand for hire purchase loans from the public sector banks who are sometimes not able to meet their loan demands in full.

The demand for chemical fertilizers and certified seeds of exotic varieties is so great that, unlike in other states, the agriculture department does not have to subsidise their distribution. Despite these favourable trends among gentlemen-farmers, the small and marginal farmers continue to follow the same old primitive method of farming.

Entrepreneurship in industrial ventures is also reportedly looking up in the wake of abundant availability of power from the Loktak project. While the district industries centres (DICs) and KVIC have been asked to draw up more schemes in the tiny and small sectors, NEITIO—the only consultancy organisation devoted to the industrial needs of the north-eastern region has been offered certain priority projects in the medium sector on a turnkey basis by the state government.

Cooperatives have been formed to start ventures requiring medium and large capital investments. In the field of electronics participation of Keltron has been obtained. It may be mentioned that the Rishang Keishing Ministry has been giving liberal incentives and taking special investment-boosting measures.

While a congenial investment climate is being created in the state, National Economic Council has made investment in a cement plant at Hundung in East District. The state government has started a starch and glucose plant at Nilakuthi, a sugar and distillery complex at Kabowakching, and a mechanised dye-house in the valley districts.

The latest banking indicators available go further to confirm that the credit-deposit ratio has touched an all-time high. No doubt, deposit accretion has marginally declined due mainly to restricted banking operations, particularly in rural areas. The ratio of advances to priority sector to total bank advances in 1982 at double the RBI-stipulated level of 40 per cent has also been significant.

The adjustment with the national price structure has not caused much grief to the consumers in this state since salary, profit-margin, farm-turnover etc. have correspondingly gone up. But the difficulties have arisen on the employment front since all the job seekers could neither be employed nor could be provided with self-employment opportunities. The worst phase of unemployment was in late Seventies when the valley's employment exchage registrations swelled to about 10 per cent of the total population of the state.

There has been, as mentioned earlier, an unabated growth in three areas. Theyare: Trade and commerce, including bulk supplies to development agencies now associated with many affluent trading houses;

Road transport where investment on the basis of bank finance has steadily gone up; and

The construction industry encompassing civil works

executed by private contractors for various infrastructural support, industrial housing or administrative and development purposes.

Fuelled by an ever-increasing profit-margin as could be expected during a demand-push inflationary spiral, business outlook has always looked bright. It did not dampen even when shutters had to be downed in the late afternoons because of frequent power supply cut, or when security was a big problem during the worst days of insurgency in 1979-80. During the Assam agitation, when rail traffic over the NEFR had been dislocated for days together, through-booking of goods from Calcutta by road was resorted to. At times, scarce goods had to be air-rushed with the extra freight.

Now the business outlook is "completely normalised" and shops and trading establishments are kept open till late in the evening with abundant power supply from the Loktak.

Trade and commerce in Manipur have, however, remained largely a one-way traffic, with only a few items (e.g. maize, cattle and forest produce) finding their market outside the state. The prodominantly agricultural structure of the state necessitates continuous import of all the other consumer goods by road either from Dimapur railway station in Nagaland along NH-39, or from Silchar in Assam along the Imphal-Silchar National Highway.

The affluence of individual road transport operators, mostly plying along the two highways, can be guessed from the fact that only the inward traffic has sustained them and rendered hire-purchase of trucks viable. Some trucks would of course ply right up to Gauhati to beat the slow-moving railway traffic across the Assam plains.

The state is witnessing a construction boom. With brick-fields facing a hard time to meet the peak demand during winter, bricks are regularly brought from Dimapur fields. Prices of all construction materials as well as the wages have shot up. Cement of course is in great demand. The authorities have allowed lifting of cement from factories outside the north eastern region rather than from Bokajan near Dimapur. Yet private parties and the state PWD almost ungrudgingly lift it by meeting the extra freight cost.

Manipur hopes to overcome industrial backwardness soon. The growth of agriculture and industries is expected to be higher in view of the generally power availability from the Loktak hydel scheme which, according to the Manipur chief minister, is "a landmark in the development programmes of this backward state."

Ninety per cent of the area of Manipur is hilly and 10 per cent valley. Sixty-five per cent of the population occupies 10 per cent area and 35 per cent is dispersed in the remaing 90 per cent area. Manipur lags far behind other states in infra-structural facilities and suffers from the imbalance of development between the hills and valley.

Agriculture being the mainstay, the plains suffer from drought and floods intermittently and the hilly area is afflicted with the problem of traditional jhum cultivation.

The state has a sizeable percentage of the population living below the poverty line. Considering a daily minium per capita calories intake of 2,400 in rural areas and 2,100 in urban areas, around 66 per cent of the rural population and 59 per cent of the urban population were estimated to be living below the poverty line in 1980-81. The per capita income of Manipur was Rs. 822 in 1979-80 as against the all-India average of Rs. 1379, at current prices.

Manipur's economy is agrarian in character. In 1971 census agriculture accounted for 71 per cent of the total workers. It fell to 67 per cent in the 1981 census when 11 per cent workers were found in household industry and 22 per cent in other activities. In terms of income generation too, the primary sector accounts for a sizeable part about 55 per cent of the total Net State Domestic Production (NSDP). The NSDP grew at an annual rate of around 4 per cent, during the Third Plan (1961-66), at 5 per cent during the period 1966-74, and at 6 per cent during the Fifth Plan period (1974-78).

Unemployment and also to some extent under-employment have been the root cause of poverty, deprivation, social unrest and tension. The number of persons on the live register of the employment exchange was 20,000 only in 1974 which rose, at the end of March 1982, to 1.36 lakh. About half of the registrants were under-matrics and the rest were matriculates and above. Presently, the Government is seized with the tremendous task of providing employment to about 67,500 persons through a programme of development in agriculture and related activities at an estimated cost of Rs. 3.77 crores in a three year period of 1982-85. The Planning Commission is working out details of the programme.

Inspite of the priority accorded to the development of transport during the last 30 years, the share of investment under five-year plans being around 72 per cent to 40 per cent from First Plan to Fourth Plan and 22 per cent to 15 per cent from Fifth Plan to Sixth Plan, the State has still a very poor transport and communications network. The National Highways No. 39 and 53 known as the New Cachar Roads are the only two roads, connecting the State with the rest of the country. Of the two, the New Cachar road is only of class IX standard and as such most of the time not usable for heavy vehicles. Above all, road is the only means of communication available in the State. Inland water transport is non-existent, except in the south district where transportation of goods from Jiribam to the southern-most subdivision of Tipaimukh is mainly accomplished by means of water transport on the river Barak.

The density of the road per 100 sq. km. of area in the State still stands at about 18 km. against about 48 km. for all-India. There are only 3,386 km. of road—1626 km. surfaced and 1760 km. unsurfaced. This excludes, of course, some roads which are outside the control of State PWD. There are still sub-divisional headquarters—Henglep, Tousem and Kasom Khullen and one District Headquarters — Chandel to be connected by an all weather black-topped road. As regards the village roads, only about 50 per cent of the 1949 villages are so far covered.

Against the Planning Commission's norm of covering 100 per cent of the villages having population above 1500 and 50 per cent of the villages having population between 1000-1500 the State has so far covered 75 of the 126 villages in the first category and 69 of the 246 villages in the second category. Most of the villages are of lower category, population size being mostly below 1000.

All the trade and commerce with the rest of the country is mostly carried through the National Highway No. 39 which connects Imphal with the rail head in Dimapur at a distance of about 205 km. All the construction and other essential materials are brought from Dimapur through Nagaland on this road. The State imports about 8,500 MT of iodised salt, 30,000 MT of rice, 24,000 MT of cement, 6,000 MT of steel, 14,000 MT of edible oils etc. per annum. In fact the total quantum of all the essential items imported per annum for public distribution by the Government alone is about 92,000 MT. The movement of these essential items are frequently disturbed due to the landslides particularly during the rainy season. Even now some portion of the National Highway No. 39 —one near Kohima and the other at 64 km. from Imphal— are yet to be firmly concreted. Due to these reasons, transportation of essential items and heavy machineries are severely handicapped. Within the State too, agricultural products produced in the remote corners, like orange in the Tamenglong area and ginger in the Timpaimukh area, cannot be transported either to the State capital or to markets outside the State. The result is that products are sold away at throw away prices and growers/producers do not receive remunerative price. Once transport is made available easily, the income of farmers/growers can be substantially increased by relatively increasing the products by ensuring a fair price.

However, the road system is not likely to be improved significantly in the near future in view of the meagre funds available. Even by the end of Sixth Plan, the State is expected to have only about 3,751 km. of road—2,161 km. surfaced and 1,590 km. unsurfaced. As it would still be difficult to improve the existing transport and communication system to a significant extent in the near future under the present trend, the Government is making efforts to improve the important roads selectively. Already improvement and construction of a number of road projects have been started under the various agencies. The NEC has also taken up improvement and construction of a number of important road projects like Tameng-long-Aizawl, Thanglon-Sinzwal-Khazwal, Ukhrul-Sangsat-Tengnoupal, etc. The NEC has also agreed in principle to take up another new road project i.e. Guite Road—from Singhat to Hanship via Singwal. This road will open many areas of the south district and will link these areas with Mizoram. When the construction and improvement of these roads including that of the New Cachar road are completed, the State's transport and communication position will considerably be improved.

The Railway Ministry has started the construction work for the extension of railway line upto Jiribam within the State of Manipur. When this railway line is constructed the State of Manipur will be put on the railway map of the country with only 1.29 km. length in Manipur.

The power shortage has been a chronic problem in Manipur. Since the Fifth Five Year Plan, the demand for electricity has been increasing tremendously but the State's power supply is inadequate till today. Against the demand of 30 MW as on March 31, 1980, the State's capacity of power supply was only 13.5 MW. The problem is further aggravated by the huge transmission and distribution losses. However, this loss has come down from 59.3 per cent in 1979-80 to 55.8 per cent in 1980-81 and to about 50 per cent in 1981-82. Of the 1,949 villages only 322 were electrified. The per capita consumption of electricity at 4.88 Kwh in 1977-78 is the lowest not only in the country (111.68 Kwh) but also in the North-Eastern Region (22.17 Kwh). Due to paucity of funds no major generation project could be taken up in the State sector and power generation efforts have been mainly confined to the installation of diesel generating sets of varying capacities of which generation cost is high. The Loktak Hydro-Electric Project with a capacity for 105 MW has been constructed at a cost of about Rs. 100 crores. The State Government has been drawing power from Assam to the tune of 5.8 MW.

Though the present level of availability of power in the State is very low there is immense scope for developing power by harnessing a number of rivers for generation of hydel power. In fact, the Loktak Hydro-Electric Project alone, produces 105 MW. In the State's own sector besides the two micro hydel schemes already commissioned, the construction of other four are also making good progress. When these projects are completed a total of about 5 MW of additional power will be available from the micro hydel projects alone. Above all 7.5 MW will also be available from Thoubal Multi-purpose Project when completed in the Seventh Plan period.

Besides the schemes mentioned above, the NEC has also taken up two micro hydel schemes, namely, Loktak Down Stream and Tuivai Hydel Project. Investigations on a number of rivers are also taken up by the State Government and the NEC. Important among them is the Tipaimukh High Dam located at Manipur and Mizoram border. The investigation has been taken up by the CWC. The expected power output is estimated at around 300 MW. When these projects are completed the State would be having abundant power for not only its use but would offer to the neighbouring States and Union Territories.

Ever since the formation of the State, Manipur has been facing a tremendous housing problem particularly for offices and residential quarters for employees at the State capital, at the district and sub-divisional headquarters. At present, many offices at the district and sub-divisional headquarters are without residential quarters. In fact, even many of the offices and its employees are also in rented buildings. The Seventh Finance Commission provided a sum of Rs. 995.371 lakhs for construction of buildings for housing judicial, police, jails, district and tribal administrative offices. Besides the above allocation, the Sixth Plan provides an outlay of Rs. 5 crores for construction of 190 functional buildings for public administration and Rs. 3 crores for construction of 633 residential quarters for government employees working in the State capital, district and sub-divisional headquarters. Till recently there were 878 residential and 286 functional buildings. These are planned to be increased to 1,511 residential buildings and 476 functional buildings at the end of the Sixth Plan period. Construction of office buildings in all the district headquarters, at least to meet the present minimum requirements has already been taken up. When these are completed, the requirement of residential accommodation for employees and also of the offices in the administrative headquarters will be improved to a great extent.

The State is a late starter in the effort for developing irrigation facilities. The severe drought of 1972 was an eye-opener and with it the first ever irrigation project—the Loktak Lift Irrigation was started at an estimated cost of Rs. 462 lakhs which had been revised to Rs.1,686 lakhs in 1980-81. Prior to this, cultivation was at the mercy of raingod and whatever little support was there, it came from some schemes under minor irrigation.

It was during the Fifth and the Sixth Plans that a beginning was made. Seven major and medium irrigation projects, namely, Thoubal Multi-purpose project, Singda Multi-purpose project, Loktak Lift Irrigation, Imphal Barrage, Khoupum Dam, Sekmai Dam and Khuga Dam have already been started. The Loktak Lift Irrigation Project was commissioned in May 1979 and now it irrigates 10,000 hectares. After its completion it will irrigate 34,000 hectares. Besides, the Imphal Barrage, the Khoupum Dam and the Sekmai Dam have provided irrigation facilities to 1000 hectares each. The total area brought under major and medium irrigation in 1981-82 was 12,000 hectares against the target of 20,000 hectares. During 1982-83 it provided irrigation facilities to 26,000 hectares and by the end of the Sixth Plan 1984-85, a total area of 49,000 hectares will be brought under irrigation.

About, 23,000 hectares were brought in 1980-81 under minor irrigation programme, mainly comprising river lift irrigation, excavation and construction of tanks, modelling and modernisation of existing channels strengthening of pucca dams, exploration of ground water etc. In 1981-82, an area of 25·66 thousand hectares, in 1982-83, 28.41 thousand hectares and by the end of the Sixth Plan (1984-85) a total area of 35 thousand hectares will be brought under minor irrigation.

Construction of some of the irrigation projects like Thoubal Project and Khuga Project will be extended into the Seventh Plan and after completion of all the projects, the ultimate irrigation potential will be 1.08 lakh hectares. By that time the state would be able to withstand the drought and would attain self-sufficiency in foodgrains.

The economy of the State, in any year so far is very much dependent on the performance in the agricultural sector. About 55 per cent of the State income is generated by this sector. Agriculture in the State, as in other States, is monsoon dependent. The distribution of rainfall in the hills varies from 2,000 to 2,500 mm except in Tamenglong where it is upto 4,017 mm and in the valley it varies from 2000 to 1,500 mm. South-west monsoon is mainly responsible for the major rainfall commencing from early part of June. About 18 per cent of the net cropped area is irrigated. Paddy and maize are the main food crops. Any irregularity in rainfall in a year affect severely its crop production and Manipur has experienced repeated droughts in the past particularly during 1972-73 and 1978-79.

More than 30 per cent of the total cropped area is in the valley which is the rice bowl of the State and under H.Y.V. crops, and improved varieties. The local hybrid seeds, Punchi and Phouibi, were introduced in 1980 and are successful in terms of productivity, and acceptance of HYV crops and modern techniques of cultivation is fast increasing. The consumption of fertilizers in the State is 11.9 kg. per hectare as against 25 kg. of all-India average. The Central Valley has high-rate of rice production of 1800 kg./hectare which is likely to reach 2,500 kg. hectare by the end of 1984-85 with the increasing use of fertilisers and larger availability of irrigation facilities.

During the Fourth Plan period with an investment of Rs. 31 crores for the State a meaningful economic development could be said to have started in Manipur. During this period some emphasis was laid on agriculture production programme on modern lines and various schemes introducing HYV programme were taken up. The original target of food-grain production at the terminal year of Fourth Plan (1973-74) at 283.85 thousand tonnes was achieved. The achievement of production of foodgrains at the end of Fifth Plan (1978-79) was 266 thousand tonnes of which rice accounted for 255 thousand tonnes. In terms of per capita availability of rice it provided 14 kg. as against the requirement of 18 kg. of rice (on the basis of NSS results of 28th Round).

Rice production during 1981-82 was 320 thousand tonnes against the target of 340 thousand tonnes showing an increase of 16.4 per cent over 1979-80 and 7.4 per cent over the preceding year. It thus provided only 16 kg. as monthly per capita availability of rice relating to production against the requirement of 18 kg. as monthly per capita consumption. This anticipated shortfall is attributed to the irregularity of rainfall during the early and later part of *Kharif* season.

Production of wheat and pulses indicates an increase of 50 per cent from that of 1980-81 while that of maize remains more or less constant. Sugarcane and oilseeds will mark respectively an increase of 9 per cent and 25 per cent over that of last year, while that of ooytion remains almost constant. In view, however, of the industrial projects in hand viz., sugar factory and spinning mill, a larger programme for development of sugarcane and cotton has been taken up.

The total net cropped area is 210 thousand hectares while the gross area is 235 thousand hectares. As regards cropping pattern, paddy is the main crop both in the valley and the hills and the fields are more or less mono-cropped. Maize is also another important *Kharif* crop in the State. But with the introduction of improved and short duration crop varieties of paddy, double cropping (paddy after paddy)has started since 1972-73 particularly in the valley areas.

The following table reveals that of the net area of 2,10,000 hectares sown during 1977-78, only 15,000 hectares (7.1 per cent) were sown more than once. The State had a vary low and perhaps erratic intensity of cropping during the years.

Cropping Intensity :

Year	Net area sown ('000 hect.)	Area sown more than once ('000 hect.)	Total area under crops ('000 hect.)	Intensity Index
1971-72	140	7	147	105.00
1972-73	140	22	162	115.71
1974-75	186	13	199	106.99
1975-76	189	12	201	106.35
1976-77	190	20	210	110.53
1977-78	210	15	225	107.14

The State's requirement of fertilizers for 1982-83 was 8,000 tonnes and the Hindustan Fertilizers Corporation of India had allotted the full requirement. The main bottleneck is the transportation of fertilisers from the nearest railway head at Dimapur from where these are to be carried by trucks through the circuitus (Dimapur - Imphal road) mountainous road of 205 km. In order to solve this problem, the Hindustan Fertilisers Corporation of India is going to establish a godown in the State and the matter is now in process with the Manipur Government. If this is set up, fertilisers can be made readily available to farmers at the time of need. Then also the problem of reaching the remote areas still persists. The State also proposed for procurement of 45 tonnes of plant protection chemicals of which 25 tonnes in technical grade are already in stock and the remaining will be procured shortly. The Tarai Development Corporation, New Delhi, will supply both *Kharif* and *Rabi* seeds. The target of producing 3,65,000 tonnes of rice in 1982-83 was achieved.

In the hills, Jhuming is extensively practised. About 60 thousand hectares of the land is estimated to be under shifting cultivation every year. Out of 2.87 lakh families about 50,000 resort to part time or full time Jhum cultivation. Shifting cultivation is on the increase as is evident from the shortening of jhuming cycle from 10 to 20 years during the past 15 to 20 years to 3 to 5 years. This has resulted in low productivity per unit area. Keeping in view the National Policy of Soil Conservation on Watershed Areas, the whole programme of soil conservation has been recast on the basis of whole village approach within selected watersheds.

The Iril Pilot Project which was started during the Fifth Plan period, has made considerable progress during the last Plan period. Under this programme 308 hectares in the watershed areas of the Iril river were brought under terrace cultivation. However, there are still quite considerable areas suitable for terracing. While encouraging farmers, free distribution of seeds and fertilisers, maintenance of irrigation channels will be extended. Only 2,160 hectares of land were under permanent cultivation during 1981-82 and 3,000 hectares under settled cultivation during 1982-83.

Manipur has tremendous potential for horticultural development. Under the various types of soil and favourable climatic conditions of the State different fruit varieties, ranging from temperate to tropical fruits grow very well. Fruits like pear, orange, pineapple and peach are abundantly found during their peak season. However, due to the lack of storage facilities, these fruits are not available throughout the year. With a massive investment, the fruit preservation factory will be expanded and this year 150 tonnes of finished fruit products will be produced.

The State has nine progeny orchards (seven in the hills and two in the valley). These progeny orchards have produced 15 lakh fruit plants during 1982-83. One hundred hectares are under cultivation. Besides, introduction and multiplication of spices, medicinal plants and oil yielding plants will be taken up in these orchards in addition to horticultural crops. A new programme which has been introduced during the Sixth Plan is the popularisation of mushroom cultivation by training the educated unemployed in rural and urban areas. A large number of shifting cultivators could be settled on the cultivation of bush crops like tea, coffee, etc. through organised sectors under Manipur Plantation Crops Corporation.

Fish is a principal food item next to rice. Fishing industries of Manipur contribute about 2 per cent of the total income of the State. However, there is a large potential for developing inland fisheries. The total water area that can be developed for fisheries is estimated at 10,000 hectares including pools, lakes and river areas etc. The majority of the people being fish consumers, the total requirement of fish in a year is about 10,000 tonnes, whereas the production is estimated at 3,000 tonnes. Therefore, large quantity of fish is imported every year from outside the State at a very high cost. With the available water resources it would not be difficult to achieve self-sufficiency in fish production by increasing fishseed production and introducing it on a large scale. During the 5th Plan (1974-78) the attainment of near self-sufficiency in fish at reasonable cost was the main objective and accordingly efforts were made to boost the production of fish. During the period, 9.17 million fingerlings were distributed, 34 fish farms were established and level of fish production reached 2,000 tonnes a year.

During the Sixth Plan period and consequent annual Plans ambitious programmes have been launched in order to increase the production of fish. For the fisheries development Rs.250 lakhs have been provided during the Sixth Plan. In 1980-81, 7 million of fingerlings were distributed and the production of fish reached 2,500 tonnes. During 1981-82, fish production rose to 3,000 tonnes.

Insufficient power and inadequate finance and lack of entrepreneurial skill have been the main bottlenecks in the establishment of industries. However, a start has been made recently. A Khandsari Sugar Factory, having a crushing capacity of 60 tonnes per day was established. This was the first medium size industry established in the State. However, there is still the problem of under-utilisation and high cost of production. During 1981-82, in fact, the mill was running only for 35 days and produced 200 quintals of sugar. The cost of production per kilogram of sugar is also about Rs. 10. The main reason for these is mostly irregular and insufficient availability of power and raw materials. This may, however, be improved during this year particularly in view of the expanding sugarcane cultivation and availability of power from Assam. Again the first phase of the training-cum-production, spinning mill of 25,250 spindles was commissioned in November 1980 with the erection of 6,912 spindles and 3,888 spindles were added in March 1982. Of this trial production is running only in 1,712 spindles. Shortage of power is holding up trial production in respect of the remaining spindles. During 1981-82 about 36.54 tonnes of yarn was produced utilising 54.64 tonnes of cotton against 99.16 tonnes of cotton imported. Since the State has not launched any scheme so far for large scale plantation of cotton, the mill will continue to depend for its raw material on external source. When all the spindles are erected and fully run the mill will require 1,750 tonnes of cotton every year and will produce 1,634 tonnes of yarn. Shortage of funds is a major problem facing the mill. The State Government is to contribute Rs. 408 lakhs as equity share capital and the remaining Rs.408 lakhs is proposed to be raised from the financial institutions. Though the IDBI sanctioned Rs. 49 lakhs as loan in 1979, the money has not been released. Moreover, no nationalised commercial bank is also coming forward. Unless their attitude changes the problem will remain unresolved.

Clearance has been given for the establishment of three

medium scale industries namely (i) sugar and distillary factory, having a crushing capacity of 1,250 tonnes per day, (ii) starch and glucose factory, having 60 tonnes per day capacity and (iii) cement factory of 50 tonnes per day capacity. However, for the sugar factory against the required sugarcane plantation area of 3,000 hectares, the present area is only about 1,400 hectares. Therefore, measures are being initiated for expanding sugarcane plantation area. Based on availability of huge bamboo area in the Barak basin and also pinewood trees in large areas in the North District preliminary studies and preparation of project report have been completed for the establishment of a pulp and paper mill. The Planning Commission has not cleared these projects so far.

The State also has a good scope for the development of sericulture since oak shrubs naturally grow in abundance in the foot-hills of the central region. Based on the survey report of the Central Silk Board, the State launched intensive oak tassar sericulture programme during the Fifth Five Year Plan. Since then steady progress is being made. As on date there are 22 grainages and 75 extension centres. Considerable importance has been given to handlooms and handicrafts because almost every house in Manipur has a loom and Manipuri women are known for their skill in handloom and handicraft work.

Apart from the above mentioned facts there are also various other industries which have a good prospect in Manipur. Among those mention may be made of cane and bamboo work, manufacture of bicycle fittings, agricultural implements, etc. These industries are less capital intensive and can be started without much difficulty as there is adequate local demand for such products. In fact action has already been taken for the establishment of an electronic project. This project is proposed to handle production of some electronic items viz. voltage stabilizer-cum-booster battery charger, battery amplifier. There is a good demand for these products in this region.

Education had a late and humble start in Manipur. In the beginning of the present century, Manipur had barely 2,658 literate persons as per the 1901 census, less than 1 per cent of the total population. The progress was also very slow. The percentage of literacy went up to 2.05 in 1911, 3.82 in 1921, 3.25 in 1931, 5.06 in 1941 and 11.41 in 1951. The trend took a sharp upward turn after independence. The literacy percentage touched 30.4 in 1961 compared with 11.41 in 1951. It was 32.9 per cent in 1971 and 42.0 per cent in 1981. In absolute terms, the number of literate persons rose from 66,000 in 1951 to 2.37 lakhs in 1961 ; from 3.53 lakhs in 1971 to 6.02 lakhs in 1981. The spectacular growth in education is a result of the implementation of the plan which accorded importance to development of education over the years. The following statement indicates the growth in number of educational institutions, scholars and teachers over a span of 25 years.

Year	Institutions	Scholars	Teachers
1955-56	1,104	93869	2932
1960-61	2,346	158859	6981
1965-66	3,130	217909	10618
1973-74	4,293	323681	15615
1977-78	4,569	339527	17294
1979-80	4,719	316958	18093

The percentage of literacy in Manipur standing at 42 (provisional) in the 1981 census is well above the corresponding all-India average of 35. In terms of enrolment at the primary and the middle stages too the State is ahead of the national average. However, the position would not be so in respect of higher education. There is also the problem of spreading education in the hilly and interior areas where there are few schools and colleges compared with comparatively heavy concentration in the valley areas.

As regards higher education, the State has few facilities. The Manipur University was established only in the Sixth Plan period and it has yet to be fully developed.

The State has high dropout rates, 81.5 per cent at primary and 85.7 per cent at middle stages. Moreover, the transfer rate of primary school children to middle school classes is very poor. To obviate the difficulties, the State Government has embarked on a plan to enrol 68,000 additional children in the primary stage and 50,000 in the middle stage as also opening of 500 preprimary education centres during the Sixth Plan. Besides, the Sixth Plan envisages to bring to school 22,500 out-of-school children in age group 6-14 years under nonformal education.

The programmes under education in the first four Five Year Plans were mainly concentrated to extending primary and middle school education. In the Fifth Five Year Plan, a start had been made for expansion of higher education.

A major programme taken up during the Fifth Plan period was the provision of school buildings for preprimary schools. A special programme based on steel tubular structure designs evolved in consultation with the Central Building Research Institute, Roorkee, was undertaken and it has proved to be a great success.

Elementary and adult education programmes have been made important ingredients of the Minimum Needs Programme so that universalisation of elementary education can be achieved at the earliest.

Besides, the programme being taken up for enhancing the availability of education facilities, diversification of education with particular reference to encouragement of science education, establishment of schools/colleges in hilly and interior areas, etc. will give a further impetus towards development of education in the State.

Manipur has only one polytechnic for imparting technical education in diploma courses in civil, electrical and mechanical engineering. In addition to the polytechnic, there were six Industrial Training Institutes with 596 seats in 1981-82. The ITIs impart training in 18 designated trades. The ITIs have a target of providing a seating capacity of 712 students by

1984-85. Moreover, the ITI at Imphal is imparting apprenticeship training. It has an intake capacity of more than 60.

There is no engineering college in Manipur. Every year about 50/60 reserved seats in various disciplines are provided by the Ministry of Education in other engineering colleges of the country. It is in this context that the State Government proposes to start one engineering college with about 80 intake capacity (40 Civil+25 Electrical +15 Mechanical) with the facilities available at the Government Polytechnic, Imphal.

Manipuri boys and girls have brought laurels to the State as well as the country at the national and even international levels. In particular, mention may be made of Shri Y. Brijen Singh who secured seven gold medals in the period from 1977 to 1981 in senior national gymnastic championships held in the country. He represented the country in the Indo-Pak Sports Meet held at Karachi in 1980 and brought gold for the country. He had been selected to represent India in the IX Asian Games. In acquatics, Kumari Y. Kiranmala Devi had a haul of more than 20 gold medals in the Indo-Srilanka-Bangladesh triangular acquatic championship in Colombo in 1979. Her performance was very good during the IX Asian Games 1982. In athletics, Kumari U. Ibemnungshi is a champion in javelin throw. She had four gold medals in short-put javelin and discus in the 20th all-India inter-state championships this year. In archery, the State started late but did well by producing national champions who represented the country in the Asiad. Manipuri girls have given a good account of themselves in football, winning national championships and representing the country in international meets. In body-building Shri N. Maipak Singh was Mr. India in 1970 and Shri Kh. Samungou Singh, Mr. Muscleman of India in 1972 represented the country in Mr. Asia and Mr. Universe contests. Other stars are Sh. Kh. Yaiskul Singh, Jr. Mr. India 1980, Sh. P. Robindro Singh, powerlifting champion in feather weight in 1977 and a number of body builders who won titles of Mr. Himalaya, Mr. Atlas of India, Mr. East India, etc. Indigenous games and adventure are built into their religion and culture. But a big problem confronting the

State is lack of adequate infrastructure for development of these activities. For this purpose the urgent need is to construct suitable stadia and sports complex and also to develop adequate facilities at district and lower levels.

The Sixth Plan (1980-85) provides an allocation of Rs. 250 lakhs for development of sports, physical training and youth services. The main programmes to be implemented during the Sixth Plan include organisation of state/district/block/rural level sports activities for participation in national level sports as also maintenance of rural sports centre, organisation of coaching camps, construction of playgrounds, giving of sports awards to talented sportsmen/sportswomen, establishment of sports school, payment of scholarships/stipends for training in sports outside the State, construction of stadium at Khuman Lampak and polo ground and also construction of mini-stadia, to mention a few.

Provision of drinking water to all sections of the population is one of the most important tasks in the State. At present, the State is not in a position to supply adequate drinking water even in urban areas comprising Imphal and a few small towns. Urban water supply schemes have been taken up in respect of Imphal, Churachandpur, Kakching, Thoubal, Bishenpur, Lmlai, Nambol and Moirang. Other small towns are being covered under rural water supply schemes. As regards urban water supply the major problem continues to be in respect of providing adequate drinking water in Imphal. The situation is obviously more serious in the rural areas, more so in the hills where villages are generally on top of the hills.

Out of 1,949 villages in the State, as many as 1,480 villages were problem and difficult villages. In terms of population, 75.32 per cent of the rural population was in these problem villages.

In respect of sources of water supply, the State has to depend on river water for all practical purposes. The difficulty in this connection is that most of the rivers have scanty water in the dry season as they are generally small rainfed rivers.

Construction materials like cement, steel and pipes are very scarce in this State. The problem is all the more acute due to transportation bottleneck. Moreover there is also the financial constraint. The State resources are inadequate to meet the need.

During 1979-80,68 problem villages were provided with potable water. The Sixth Plan has set a target of providing water facilities to 894 problem villages by 1984-85. In 1980-81, 34 problem villages and in 1981-82, 312 such problem villages were covered leaving a balance of 968 problem villages to be covered in the subsequent years.

The national target is to cover all the remaining problem villages by 1985 excepting in some difficult areas like hilly and desert regions. In order to enable the State take up this important task, the Government of India is expected to release grants totalling Rs. 5.23 crors to the State Government during the Sixth Plan period under the Centrally Sponsored Accelerated Rural Water Supply Programme to supplement the State programme.

The good effects of implementation of the health programes are being felt in the health and strength of the Manipuris. The number of doctors, nurses and other medical personnel in the State has remarkably increased from 55 doctors and 167 nurses, midwives and dais in 1965 to 360 doctors and 516 nurses, midwives and dais in 1979. Hospitals, dispensaries, P.H.Cs, sub-centres and other medical and health institutions as also infrastructure for medical care of the people have since been improved tremendously. The population per doctor had come down from 15,711 in 1960-61 to 3,831 in 1979. Similarly, the population per bed which was 1,944 in 1960-61 had improved to 1,022 in 1976. In respect of nursing services, nurse doctor ratio which was 3.04 in 1965 came down to 1.44 in 1979, nurse bed ratio from 3.08 beds per nurse in 1965 to 2.59 in 1979, and 5366 persons per nurse in 1965 to 2573 in 1979. The death rate, according to the estimates of the Sample Registration Services (SRS) has been 6.3 per thousand in 1977. Contagious and communicable diseases have been effectively controlled. The longevity of the life has risen from 32 years in 1951 to more than 50 years at present. By the end of 1979-80, 115 PHSCs could serve about 23,000 persons in the valley and about 5,000 in the hills. By the end of 1979-80, there were 25 PHCs—17 in the hills and eight in the valley. This provided one P.H.C. for every one lakh persons in the valley and for every 30,000 persons in the hills. Similarly, in respect of rural hospitals for referal services in the rural and hill areas, there were already five such hospitals by the end of 1979-80. Of these, two are in the hill areas and three in the valley.

The next stage of referal services was the establishment of 30 to 100 bedded district hospitals depending upon the size of the district and its population. By the end of 1979-80, there were six district hospitals—five in the hills and one in the valley in addition to five upgraded rural hospitals. In respect of the control of communicable diseases the State achieved considerable progress. By the end of 1979-80 already five T.B. clinics and three leprosy control units and T.D. centres were established.

The Sixth Plan further seeks to improve the medical and health facilities for the people. A massive effort is being made to provide a Primary Health Centre for every 60,000 persons and a Primary Health Sub-centre for every 5,000 persons in the valley and a Primary Health Centre for every 25,000 persons and Primary Health Sub-Centres for every 5000 persons in the hills. The Plan envisages one Rural Hospital for about four PHCs. The Sixth Plan has the target of having 11 Rural Hospitals, 40 PHCs and 399 PHSCs in the State.

Family welfare programme is being implemented in the State on voluntary basis.

The Manipur Government's Fruit Preservation Factory in Imphal produced 200 tonnes of fruit products this year, thereby almost tripling its production in 1982-83.

The products of this factory are mainly pine-apple juice squash, slices, etc.

Further expansion of the factory with the installation of a

boiler and modern equipment promises a production target of 300 tonnes in the coming year.

Arrangements have already been made to export 50 tonnes of pine-apples from Manipur to the Soviet Union.

Foodgrains production in Manipur rose by 9,000 tonnes to 3,58,000 tonnes in 1982-83 in spite of devastating floods, unsually widespread attack of pests and heavy hailstorms.

Yet it fell short of the target by about 25,000 tonnes.

Vigorous efforts are afoot to raise a still better crop during 1983-84. Rice, maize, wheat and pulses being the main foodcrops of the State, hybrid seeds of these are being made available to farmers. New varieties of paddy have been sown in 6,660 hectares so that two crops can be raised there. About 8000 tonnes of fertilisers have been distributed to the farmers. At 33 kg per hectare, fertiliser consumption in Manipur is among the highest among the North-Eastern States.

The insect pest problem which is chronic to the State is more or less under control now, thanks to the introduction of modern pesticides and weedicides.

In addition to the existing 400 community paddy nurseries, a subsidy of Rs. 1500 is granted to each farmer to start his own paddy nursery. This is expected to help encourage more area under double cropping and help timely replantation in water scarcity areas. When the 300 acre Regional Seed Production Centre becomes operational shortly, the State is expected to become self-sufficient in foundation seeds.

Potato production has also progressed very much. The Regional Seed Potato Farm, Mao, is now able to supply disease-resistent varieties of seed to neighbouring States. Last year 16000 kg. of seed potato was supplied to Nagaland.

Pulses and oilseeds also are receiving due attention. During the current financial year 12000 hactares of new land will be brought under pulses. Oilseeds will be grown in 16000 hactares of newly reclaimed land.

Prospects of becoming self-sufficient in foodgrains have become bright for Manipur during the current financial year.

In Manipur, 175 school textbooks for tribals have been

published, and educational equipments have been supplied to 400 schools in backward areas as part of the State Government's vigorous effort to improve the condition of the economically backward people of the State.

Stipends are being provided to 150 tribal students. Another 200 students receive stipends to pursue higher studies in industry and trade. Moreover, some 350 Tribal Societies and Organisations are given financial assistance to revive various tribal arts and cultural performances. More hostels and schools are being constructed in the hilly areas for the benefit of tribal students.

The Manipur Tribal Development Corporation has been provided with Rs. 20 lakhs as share capital and money. With the help and technical assistance from HUDCO and financial institutions, the Corporation hopes to execute housing schemes for middle and lower income groups of tribals.

A unique feature of the health scheme for the tribal people is the financial assistance they get to undergo treatment, both inside and outside the State. Godowns are being constructed at nine strategic places so that basic necessities could be made available to the tribal people without any hardship.

Manipur is marching towards economic prosperity with leaps and bounds and has reached almost on the threshold of overall development. With economic development changes are also bound to take place in social and cultural fields. The work also depicts the eco-cultural transformation of the State in the recent years.

APPENDICES

APPENDIX-I

Origin of the Manipuris

THE origin of the Manipuris is obscure, and the written records, having been mostly composed since they became Hindus, are not worthy of much credit. Their claim to a Hindu origin has been rejected by Pemberton, who considers them to be the descendants of a Tartar colony which probably emigrated from the north-west border of China during the sanguinary conflicts for supremacy which took place between the several members of the Chinese and Tartar dynasties in the Thirteenth and Fourteenth centuries, at which time there was an extensive kingdom called Pong, occupying the country between the frontier of Yunnan and the hills separating the Kubbo valley from Manipur, extending north apparently to the mountains which bound Assam on the south-east and south, as far down as the parallel of 23° 35′. In the records of Manipur, however, their history is traced from the 30th year of the Christian era down to the year 1714, in which period they number a succession of 47 kings, the average length of whose reign is thus made to amount to upwards of 35 years. In this long period we have but one event of any importance recorded, said to have taken place in the year 1475, during the reign of the Raja Kyamba, when the refractory tributary of Khumbat, at that time dependent upon the kings of Pong, was attacked and expelled from his territory by the united forces of Pong and Manipur, and the Kubbo valley was formally annexed to the latter country, in virtue of an alliance which had then taken place between a daughter of Kyamba of Manipur and the king of Mogoung, the capital of the Pong dominions. From 1475 to 1714, the date of accession of the Raja Gharib Newaz or Pam Haibaba, nothing of any importance is recorded in the meagre annals of Manipur. From this period we find the people assuming a position of peculiar interest : emerging from their mountain strongholds, they wage war successfully in the fertile valley of the Irrawaddy, attack and reduce the most important Burmese towns and villages on the banks of the Mu, Chindwin and Irrawaddy rivers, and at last plant their standard in the capital itself. The truth of this portion of their historical annals receives most unexpected and satisfactory corroboration from the records of Ava, in which all the principal circumstances are narrated nearly as we find them in the chronicles of Manipur, with a trifling variation of three or four years in the dates assigned to them, for the knowledge of which we are indebted to the researches of Lieutenant Colonel Burney, the Resident at Ava. Very shortly after Gharib Newaz ascended the throne, he commenced that career of conquest which we find recorded in the Burmese annals. In 1725 he attacked and defeated Burmese force at the mouth of the Maglang river; the following year repulsed an army of 30,000 men, which had penetrated into the valley, and captured three divisions. In 1735 he crossed the Ningthee river, attacked and destroyed the town of Myedu, on the banks of the Mu river, and carried off numerous captives. Two years subsequently he successively defeated two Burmese armies, amounting to 7,000 foot, 700 horse, and 20 elephant, and devastated the whole country from banks of the Khodung Choung to Dabayen. In 1738 he again crossed the Ningthee river, attacked and dispersed a Burmese army of 15,000 foot, 3,000 horse, and 30 elephant ; and at the termination of the rains of the same year, at the head of a force of 20,000 men, marched between the Burmese army, three divisions of which occupied the towns of Matsen, Dabayen and Myedu, and, to use the language of the Burmese historians, "without stopping" attacked and carried the stockaded positions around the ancient capital of Sagaing of which he obtained possession. Religious fanaticism appears to have stimulated the Manipuris to this last act of successful daring; for the Burmese chronicles record the name of a Brahmin who is said to have assured them that they would be preserved from all evil by drinking and bathing in the waters of the Irrawaddy river. In 1739, Gharib Newaz, aided, it is said, by the Cacharis, again invaded Ava with a force of 20,000 men; but failing in an attack on a Burmese force, stockaded at Myedu, he was deserted by his allies, and, after suffering much loss, was compelled to retire to the strongholds of his own country. He appears to have remained inactive on the frontier until the year 1749, when he again crossed the Ningthee river, and marching along its left bank with an army of 20,000 foot and 3,000 horse, encamped near the confluence of the Chindwin and Irrawaddy rivers, waiting for a favourable opportunity to cross the latter river and attack the capital. The most formidable preparations were made to oppose him, and he appears to have been shaken from his purpose by one of those trifling incidents which, to the superstitious mind of the savage, are proofs of the will of Heaven. During the night his standard was blown down, and, under the influence of this sinister omen, he was glad to negotiate rather than to fight, and, presenting a daughter about 12 years of age to the king of Ava, immediately returned and commenced a retreat by the road of Myedu to his country. Near the Mu river he was attacked by the Koees, a fierce tribe belonging to that part of the country, whom he quickly subdued, and resuming his journey reached the Maglang river, called by the Burmese the Yoo-Choung. Here he was met by his son Oogut Shah, or Kakeelalthaba, who upbraided him with the unsuccessful termination of his expedition, and with having tendered homage to the king of Ava by the presentation of his daughter. The result of these remonstrances was that Gharib Newaz was deserted by all but 500 men, with whom he again retired, for the avowed purpose of soliciting aid from the king of Ava against his rebellious son. He resided for a short time at Tasingain, and gave a daughter in marriage to the Toungoo Raja, under whose protection he remained until Ava was destroyed by the Peguers; when in an attempt to re-enter Manipur, he was met by the emissaries of Oogut Shah at the mouth of the Maglang river, and cruelly murdered, together with his eldest son, Shamshaee, and all the principal men of the court who had shared his compulsory exile. Oogut Shah was, however, soon expelled from the throne by his brother, Burut Shah, who was raised to the regal dignity by the unanimous voice of his subjects. He reigned but two years, and on his death, was succeeded by Gouroosham, the eldest son of Shamshaee, an act of justice by which the direct succession of the line was again restored.

The victorious career of Gharib Newaz clearly proves that during his reign the Manipuris had acquired very considerable power ; and as the events just narrated are drawn almost exclusively from Burmese historical works, and are the acknowledgments of a defeated enemy, all suspicion of their truth must cease to exist. With Gharib Newaz the power of Manipur seems to have entirely deserted her; very shortly after his death, the first great invasion of the country by a Burmese army, commanded by a relative of Alompra, took place in 1755; and this is known in Manipur at the present day as the "Koolthakahalba," or primary devastation, and is rendered the more remarkable as being the first occasion on which the Burmese appear to have owed their success entirely to the use of firearms, their weapons, like those of the Manipuris, having up to this period consisted almost entirely of the dhao, spear, and bow and arrow. In 1758, Alompra in person undertook the conquest of this devoted country, and, proceeding up the Chindwin with a fleet of boats, laid waste its western bank which was inhabited by the Kathay Shans, or Shans tributary to Manipur, where he disembarked, and, crossing the Ungoching hills by the Khumbat route, marched through Kubbo, and entered the Manipur valley by the Imole pass at Palel. He was here met by the Manipuris under Burut

Shah, and, after a sanguinary conflict, proved victorious. He remained thirteen days in possession of the capital, and intelligence being then received of the revolt of the Peguers, he returned with the utmost expedition to Ava.

The invasion of Manipur by Alompra must have been most disastrous to the inhabitants of that country, as they then, for the first time, sought external aid, and appeared a few years afterwards as supplicants for British protection. Oogut Shah, having been expelled from the throne two years before the invasion of Alompra, appears from the communications of Mr. Verelst, who was then Chief at Chittagong, in the course of the year 1762, to have endeavoured to interest the British Government in his behalf, and by representing himself as unjustly driven from the throne had created a feeling of sympathy for his misfortunes. Jaee Sing, brother of Gouroosham, who was then in Manipur, becoming acquainted with these negotiations, deputed a confidential messenger, named Hurree Doss Gossein, with a letter to Mr. Verelst, in which the real character of his uncle and the crimes of which he had been guilty were depicted. Of the truth of these statements, the Tripurah Raja appeared perfectly satisfied, and the British authorities not only withdrew from any further communication with Oogut Shah, but prepared to support Jaee Sing against his machinations and the aggressions of the Burmese.

A treaty of alliance, offensive and defensive, was negotiated on the 14th September 1762 with Hurree Doss Gossein, on behalf of his master Jaee Sing, by Mr. Verelst, in which the aid of a contingent of British troops was promised, whenever the Raja might find it expedient to attempt the recovery of such portions of his territory as had been wrested from him by the Burmese ; and he promised, in return, to make such grants of land to the English as might suffice for the establishment of a factory and fort, and a distance of country round such factory and fort, of 8,000 cubits, free of rent for ever. He was further to afford every facility for the prosecution of the trade with China, and when put in possession of the Burmese country by the six companies of sepoys whose aid had been promised, he was to indemnify the English for the injuries they had sustained at Negrais and in Pegu from Burmese violence and treachery.

No communication appears to have been received from Jaee Sing, when the troops destined for the enterprise started from Chittagong early in January 1763. Marching by routes along the eastern frontier of Bengal, they reached Casspoor, the then capital of the Cachar country, in the month of April, when they suffered severely from heavy rain, which had continued to fall from the 21st of March ; their progress to Manipur was, in consequence, arrested, and finding Casspoor unhealthy, they were compelled to return to Jeynugur, a pergunnah on the left bank of the Barak river at the eastern foot of the Telyn hill. Circumstances of a political nature rendering the recall of the force necessary, a letter was despatched to Mr. Verelst, who returned with it to Chittagong. The treaty had been conveyed to Manipur by Hurree Doss, for the information of Jaee Sing ; but some change in the administration of that country must have taken place, for in October of the following year, three accredited agents arrived at Chittagong, deputed by Gouroosham, who is represented as again in possession of the regal power ; he confirms the treaty entered into with Jaee Sing, but states his inability to pay, in specie of gold or silver, the expense incurred by the troops to be employed in his service, the Burmese having destroyed a great part of the dominions of Meklee ; he agrees, however, to refund whatever sums may have been already expended by the British Government on his account, and to repay, in the produce of his country, the charges for military assistance. As an earnest of the sincerity of his intentions, he makes an immediate offer of 500 Meklee gold rupees, to be valued at 12 silver rupees each. Allusion is also made in this document to the gold mines on the banks of the Burhampooter, in the dominions of Meklee, as well as any other mines of gold, silver, lead, iron, tin, copper, and precious stones which were known to exist, or might hereafter be recovered.

With this treaty all communication between the British and Manipuri authorities appears to have ceased. The death of Gouroosham, with whom it had been concluded, soon followed and Jaee Sing had resumed the reins of government but for a short time, when another invasion of the Burmese under Schembegwen in 1765, overwhelmed his unhappy country. The Manipuris were defeated, Jaee Sing fled into Cachar, and the horrors of captivity were superadded to the sufferings inflicted upon them by their relentless enemies. As soon as the Burmese had retired, which they did after raising a man remotely connected with the royal family, called Eeringha, to the throne, Jaee Sing returned, and dispossessed the usurper, whose life was spared. From 1765, the date of the last great invasion mentioned by Symes, Jaee Sing had been actively engaged in attempts to restore the country to some degree of prosperity, and his efforts would appear to have been but too successful, as the knowledge of its improved condition promised a fresh harvest of slaves and cattle and stimulated the Burmese to renew their aggressions. Their forces advanced in two divisions one of which proceeding by water devastated the villages on the western bank of the Ningthee river while the other, penetrating through the valley of Kubbo, their united forces entered the Manipur valley and were met by the troops of Jaee Sing near Lungthabol. A bloody conflict, which lasted for three days, terminated in the total discomfiture of the Manipuris, and Jaee Sing fled across the hills into Assam. The Burmese raised the Moirang Raja to the vacant throne, and returned to their own country. Jaee Sing having obtained assistance in Assam, and relying on the attachment of the people, again returned to Manipur, devastated Moirang, and resumed the government of his country. Between 1775 and 1782, Jaee Sing had made no less than four successful attempts to regain his throne, but was as often expelled by a fresh Burmese force, and on each occasion was compelled to fly into Cachar, where he obtained a temporary refuge. In 1782, he, however, appears to have made some compromise with his enemies, and from that period until 1798 he seems to have been allowed to remain in quiet possession of his devastated country. In January of that year, he left his eldest surviving son, Robinchundruh, in charge of Manipur, and set out on a pilgrimage to Nuddea. Distrusting the Cachar Raja, who refused him a passage through his territories, he travelled towards Tipperah, and, giving a daughter in marriage to the Raja of that country, resumed his journey and died near Bhagovangola on the banks of the Ganges in October 1799. From this period the history of Manipur presents an unvarying scene of disgusting treachery between the numerous sons of Jaee Singh, who, in their contests for supremacy, arrayed the unhappy people of the country in hostile warfare against each other, and inflicted miseries upon them, little if at all inferior to those they had suffered at the hands of their common enemy and the Burmese. Of these sons, Robinchundruh, the eldest, who had been left in charge of the country by his father, was murdered in 1801. Modochundruh, the next in succession, shared the same fate in 1806. When Choorjet Sing ascended the throne, his brother Marjeet almost immediately afterwards conspired against him, but, being unsuccessful in an attack, fled to Wuqueel and supplicated assistance from the king of Ava, who despatched at Tummoo to Manipur on his behalf, and he was pardoned by Choorjet. Received into favour, he again rebelled, and, being repulsed in two attacks upon the capital, fled into Cachar, from whence, with a few followers, he made his way to Ava through the province of Arakan. In this country he remained six or seven years, and at the end of that time, in 1812, succeeded in inducing the king of Ava to espouse his cause, and to place him on the throne of Manipur, for which he agreed to renounce all claim on the Kubbo valley, and to acknowledge his dependence on the king of Burma. To the friendship of the monarch of Ava was he indebted for the interest shown on his behalf; and it will be subsequently seen how he requited the good offices of his young protector. In the cold weather of 1812, a considerable army marched from the Burmese territory to establish Marjeet on the throne of Manipur. At Tummoo, in the Kubbo valley, two divisions were formed, one of which, accompanied by Marjeet Sing, entered Manipur by the Imole pass, and debouched in the valley near Kokshingkhoolel; second, under, the Samjok Raja, entered by the Muchee route, and encamped near Hueerok. This division was totally routed, and its leader killed by Petumber Sing, a nephew of the Raja Choorjet Sing, who, with the main army, had advanced to Kokshing. A conflict, which lasted for five days, terminated in his discomfiture; he fled into Cachar with a few of his followers, and the country submitted to the yoke of the usurper. Marjeet, at the expiration of ten days, dismissed his Burmese friends, and continued for five years in undisturbed possession of the country. During this period, Manipur is represented as having regained almost all its former prosperity. The friendship existing with the Court of Ava tended to encourage trade. The prosperity of the inhabitants was proved in numerous herds of buffaloes and bullocks which grazed in the plains, and a considerable accession of people had taken place from the return of those who had accompanied Marjeet in his flight. Marjeet and his principal officers had, from their long residence in Ava, adopted many of the luxurious habits of that Court, and they affected a degree of splendour in dress and the equipments of their horses which contrasted very strikingly with their former simplicity. Nothing, however, but terror of the Burmese could have induced the principal families in Manipur to tolerate the presence of Marjeet, whose sanguinary disposition was early shown in the execution of almost all Choorjet's followers and the attempted murder of many of his nephews. In 1818 he invaded Cachar with a large force, which penetrated the hills in three divisions, and would have effected the conquest of that country with ease, had its Raja, Gobindchunder, not interested Choorjet Sing in his favour. This prince had been residing for some time at Jynteea, and, on learning the situation of affairs in Cachar, immediately came to Govindchunder's assistance; and Marjeet, hearing of his arrival, was so much afraid of his influence amongst the Manipuris, that he made a precipitate retreat across the hills into his own country. Choorjet with the assistance of Gumbheer Sing, succeeded in obtaining possession of the greater portion of the Cachar territory, in which he finally established himself with all his followers.

In 1819, when the king of Ava ascended the throne, it was determined to commemorate the event with an unusual degree of splendour, and all the tributary princes, as is customary on such occasions, were summoned personally to do homage to the new sovereign. Amongst others, Marjeet Sing of Manipur was ordered to attend, and as it was to the friendly exertions of this very king that he was entirely indebted for his present position, it was natural to suppose that such a summons would have been gladly obeyed. Some circumstances, however, such as the forcible cutting of timber in the Kubbo valley, and the erection of a richly-gilded palace, had been the subject of remonstrance from the Court of Ava a short time before ; and distrusting their intention, Marjeet declined obeying the order for his apperance at the installation of the king ; but anxious to avert the consequences of a more explicit refusal, he pleaded the hostile intentions of his brothers in excuse for his disobedience. A Burmese army was immediately despatched to seize the rebel ; they were encountered by the Manipuris at Kokshing, the scene of many former struggles between the same troops, and the contest was at length terminated by the retreat of Marjeet, who, deserting his troops, fled precipitately towards Cachar, followed by so large a proportion of the population of the country that the Burmese gained little more by their conquest than the glory of having vanquished a force greatly inferior in numbers. Marjeet, on reaching Cachar, was kindly received by his brother Choorjet to whom he made a formal resignation of the regal authority, by giving into his charge the sacred images of Govinduh and Burnamchundruh, which he had brought away with him from Manipur. Heerachundruh, the son of Robinchundruh and nephew of Marjeet, continued at the head of a small body of horse to annoy the Burmese garrison left in Manipur, who in vain attempted to capture him. He was secretly supported by his countrymen, who admired his gallantry, and by keeping him acquainted with the movements of the enemy, enabled him to cut off many of their small detachments.

In 1822, Petumbhur Sing, another nephew, was despatched from Cachar by Choorjet to his assistance, and they succeeded in drawing a large Burmese detachment into an ambuscade every man of which was cut to pieces. The country had been so much devastated by the long continuance of hostilities, that the leaders of these parties found themselves unable to sustain the force they kept up, and consequently withdrew into Cachar. In the following year Petumbhur Sing was again detached by Choorjet to depose a man called Shoobol, who had been placed on the gaddi by the Burmese, and having effected that object Petumbhur assumed the dignity himself. To dispossess him, Gumbheer Sing left Cachar with a small force, and Petumbhur having been worsted in an action near Jeynugur, fled to the Court of Ava, where he remained. Gumbheer Sing, from the extreme difficulty of obtaining supplies, was compelled to return almost immediately to Cachar, when, in consequence of disagreements with his brother Choorjet the latter retired to Sylhet, leaving Marjeet and Gumbheer in possession of nearly the whole of that territory of which Govindchundruh had been unjustly deprived. In this state of affairs the Burmese war commenced ; the forces of Ava again occupied Manipur, and when our frontier was threatened through Cachar, negotiations were opened with the three Manipuri brothers, who supplicated to be taken under our protection. The proposition was acceded to, and the Burmese authorities, though made acquainted with the fact, persisted in their original design of invading it, and eventually overran the province with a very considerable body of troops. Gumbheer Sing, the most enterprising of the three brothers, with whom we had negotiated, raised from among his own followers a body of 500 men, who actively co-operated with our troops in expelling the Burmese force from Cachar ; and in June 1825 he compelled them to evacuate the Manipur valley. In the following year, having obtained some reinforcements, he entered Kubbo, attacked the Burmese forces in their stockaded position at Tommoo, and pursuing them across the Ungoching hills, cleared the western bank of the Ningthee river of every opposing detachment. At the conclusion of the peace by the treaty of Yandaboo in February 1826, Gumbheer Sing was recognised as the Raja of Manipur, where he continued to reign until January 1834, when he suddenly expired, leaving an infant son, the Raja Kirti Singh, who was formally acknowledged by the British Government, and a regency, of which the Sunaputtee, Nar Sing, his late father's most confidential and faithful friend, governed the country. During the regency of Nar Sing, numerous attempts were made to upset the government. The first occurred in 1838. In that year Tarring Komba, eldest son of a former Raja Robinchundruh, made a raid with 300 followers from Cachar. They were met by 500 men of Nar Sing on entering the valley of Manipur. In the fight which ensued, Tarring Komba and his brother, with many followers, were killed, 100 were taken prisoners, the remainder fled. The prisoners were released after being detained for one year. Within the next few years the following attempts at securing the raj took place : Marjeet's eldest son named Jogendra Sing, tried to invade the country ; but he and his brother were both killed in the hills on their way to the valley. Two sons of Choorjet Sing, Tribhubunjet and Ram Sing, also made an attempt ; they managed to get inside the Raja's enclosure at night, but in the fight which ensued in the morning both were killed. After Nar Sing had declared himself Raja, another attempt was made, not long before his death, by one Melai Ramba and his brother, descendants of Raja Churai Ramba. They invaded the valley from Cachar. In an engagement which took place in the valley, Melai Ramba's brother was killed and himself taken prisoner ; he was executed by being put into a basket and flung into the river. This was the last political execution. It will be readily understood that these continued disturbances and fights rendered the position of the Political Agent anything but pleasant ; however, he was never interfered with, although sometimes rather awkwardly situated, as when, in the progress of one of the skirmishes, a cannon ball coming from the Raja's enclosure struck his house. On the Rani reaching Cachar, as before mentioned, she placed herself under British protection, and had a small guard of sepoys for her security. An allowance of Rs. 100 a month was allowed her from the Kubbo compensation money for her and the young Raja's support. During a stay of five years in Cachar, she made many applications to Government to regain the gadi for the Raja ; but these were not listened to, Nar Sing having become Raja. She then proceeded to Assam with a view of consulting with Captain Jenkins, the Commissioner, who she supposed would be able to aid her in her efforts to regain the gadi for her son. Some correspondence went on, it is believed, on the subject, but the Rani was finally referred to the Manipur Political Agent. After remaining one year in Assam, she returned with the Raja to Cachar, where she remained until the death of Nar Sing in 1850. After the death of Nar Sing, which took place from cholera, an epidemic of that disease then raging in the valley, his brother Debendra Sing, a man of less firmness and talent than Nar Sing, assumed the raj, it is said in the Political Agent's correspondence of the time, at the request of Nar Sing. He is said also to have exhorted his three sons to proceed to Cachar and render every assistance in their power to further this end. Be this as it may, there is no doubt that the three sons of Nar Sing, almost immediately after his death, fled to Cachar, and put themselves in communication, together with other influential men who had left Manipur, with Chandra Kirti Sing. Fearing disturbances after the flight of Nar Sing's sons to Cachar, a guard was placed over the Raja Chandra Kirti Sing. About this time the Raja petitioned for the restoration of his raj ; but before he had time to receive an answer, he had contrived to elude his guards, and was in full march for Manipur, accompanied by Nar Sing's three sons and about 100 followers. Halting at the Jiri river, where he was joined by more recruits, he sent a letter to the Political Agent, intimating his intentions of coming on to Manipur. He met with but little opposition on the way, and reached the valley safely. After another trifling skrimish, he established himself in a former residence of the Raja situated three miles from the capital to the south and commanding the most fertile part of the valley. During five days matters remained quiet; many of the followers of Debendra Sing deserted him and went over to the young Raja, whose advent was apparently approved of by the majority of the people. After this period, Debendra Sing's prospects became hopeless, and he was forced to fly, after having been attacked by the trops who had up to this time adhered to his cause. Debendra Singh made his way with his family to Cachar, where he remained, making no doubt preparations for the attempts he afterwards made to recover the raj. It would appear, both from the opinions of the then Political Agent and the present statements of the Manipuris, that Debendra Singh was not popular, and that, when a son of Gumbheer Sing appeared on the scene, the prestige of his being the only male descendant of the Raja, who had freed the country from the hated Burmese told immensely in his favour. The fact of Chandra Kirti Sing having been accompanied in his expedition by Nar Sing's sons had also a favourable effect, as tending to unite the two great factions of the country—the supporters of Gumbheer Singh's family and that of Nar Sing. Debendra Sing having fled after only occupying the gadi for three months, Chandra Kirti Sing assumed the raj, naming as joboraj, or successor, the eldest son of Nar Sing, another son, to be senaputi. The attitude of the Political Agent at this period was of simple expectancy, and, with the exception that the Kubbo compensation money was withheld, nothing was done. He stated, as his opinion, that the above arrangement with Nar Sing's son was not likely to continue, and feared that, from his ignorance of the country, the young Raja would fall entirely into the hands of his advisers. Not more than a fortnight had elapsed after the flight of Debendra Sing, when disturbances, broke out. A younger brother of Debendra who had remained behind on his flight, united with Nar Sing's sons, and with 600 followers attacked the Raja; but they were defeated, and fled towards Cachar. When Debendra Sing assumed the raj, apparently by desire of Nar Singh, the Political Agent recommended that he should be recognised by Government. This recognition was accorded; but as it arrived eleven days after Debendra's flight, it could not be acted on, and was not made known. Before the above orders were received, however, and to add to the complications of the situation, Debendra Sing had made known his intentions of making an attempt to recover the raj. The first attempt was made about two months after his flight from Manipur, and was unsuccessful, his adherents being dispersed by the Raja's troops in the hills about halfway to Manipur. Another attempt was made after this, but was defeated by Government sepoys, who followed up and dispersed the raiders. After the last raid, Debendra Sing was seized by the Cachar officials, and conveyed first to Sylbet, and afterwards to Dacca, where he died in November 1871. He was supported by an allowance from the Kubbo compensation money of Rs. 70 a month. In the meantime, matters in Manipur were going on from bad to worse, and great oppression was caused by the reckless behaviour of the authorities, unchecked apparently by the Raja. These unscrupulous men, fearing the success of Debendra Sing's plans for regaining the raj, only thought of enriching themselves at the expense of the unfortunate inhabitants, who by this time had become so dissatisfied with the rule of Chandra Kirti Sing that the majority of them would have gladly welcomed back Debendra Sing, who would doubtless have succeeded in reaching the valley in his second attempt, had he not been attacked and routed by the British forces. Not content with oppressing the people, the attitude of the Raja and his advisers was at this period one of decided hostility to the Political Agent, who was accused unjustly, it need scarcely be said, of keeping back the Kubbo compensation allowance, which the Raja and his harpies constantly clamoured for, and which was withheld until it could be clearly shown that the Raja was able to hold his own. So insolent had they become, although they had been assured that the Political Agent, in withholding the Kubbo allowance, was only acting up to the orders of Government, that they openly gave out that, if they did not receive the allowance when the next instalment became due, they would reoccupy the Kuboo valley. The whole of the conduct of the Manipur Government at this time is characterized by the Political Agent as being "unbecoming from the Court of the son of the man who owed his throne to the British Government". The Political Agent, writing to Government at this time, states: "I have met with some petty acts of annoyance indicating a bad spirit in the authorities, who (at least many of them) seem to think that the presence of the representative of the British Government ought to be no check on them; that by their prowess they gained the throne for the young Raja in spite of the British Government and now they have got it, they may do exactly as they choose. I trust, however, as they cool down, they may understand their position. The young Raja, I believe, does." Again, in October 1850, the Political Agent fears that the unsettled state of the country may induce the Burmese to interfere and assist a prince named Nibirjit, who was then in high favour with the Court of Ava. In December 1850, matters at length reached a climax demanding interference. At this time, it was clearly shown that the Manipur Government had supplied arms and men to a tribe of Nagas to the north at that time hostile to the British Government. All the remonstrances of the Political Agent failed in eliciting any satisfactory explanation of this transaction, and the matter was reported to Government. In reply, Government administered a rebuke to the Manipur Raja, and reminded him that his State only existed by the sufferance and countenance of the British Government. At this the state of affairs improved considerably, the Raja evidently being recalled to a proper sense of his position, and ruling with a greater regard to the rights and feelings of his subjects.

In February 1851, the orders of Government recognising the succession of Chandra Kirti Sing to the raj of Manipur were conveyed to him, and shortly afterwards another assurance of stability was given by Government undertaking still further to guarantee the raj to him and his descendants, and to prevent, by force of arms if necessary, any attempts by rival chiefs to dislodge him. Very shortly after the above recognition, other raids on Manipur took place, which are related briefly as follows.

In 1851, Debendra Sing's sons made an attempt. In the subsequent fight which ensued, Debendra Sing's eldest son was killed and two of Nar Sing's sons taken prisoners; they were afterwards made officials and forgiven. One year after the above, two sons of Madu Chandra and one of Marjeet Sing's, named Kanai Sing, made an attempt. Madu Chandra's two sons were captured, and afterwards died in Manipur; Kanai Sing escaped, and subsequently made other attempts. Up to the time of the outbrack of the Indian mutiny of 1857, no other raids took place. At the latter end of 1857, or beginning of 1858, the sepoys stationed at Chittagong mutinied and made for Cachar; they were met and defeated at Latu on the borders of the Sylhet and Cachar districts by a detachment of the Sylhet Light Infantry, now the 44th Native Infantry; they afterwards continued on their way east in the direction of the Manipur frontier. The Political Agent, on hearing of the Chittagong mutiny, asked the Raja to send a body of his troops to the frontier to prevent the mutineers entering his country; this was at once done, and 400 men under two majors despatched. These troops did good service, and captured a number of the mutineers, who were given up to the British officials. It is supposed that nearly, if not all the mutineers, were killed, captured, or perished miserably in the jungles of the Manipur and Kuki hills. During the whole of the period of the mutiny, the Political Agent, in his reports to Government, states that the conduct and feelings of the Raja and the majority of the officials and inhabitants were at that time good, and the Raja's offers of assistance to the British Government, in case of need, sincere. Advantage was taken of the arrival of the mutineers by some of the Manipuri chiefs in Cachar, and several joined them, with a view of getting their aid in overthrowing the Manipur Government. Among them was Nurendrojit or Chai Aham ("Chai Aham', three years, so called as he was supposed to have been three years in his mother's womb), a younger son of Choorjet Sing's; he was made prisoner and handed over to the British officers; he was eventually transported.

During the mutiny, an attempt was made by Government to enlist men as sepoys for general service; but it quite failed, as the Manipuris did not like the idea of serving in the North-Western Provinces, more especially as disturbances were still going on. In 1859, at the recommendation of the Political Agent, the Raja was presented with a dress of honour, sword, and belt; at the same time, eight of his chief officers received khilluts. These gifts were expressive of approval of the conduct of the Raja and his officers during the mutiny. One Major Roma Sing alro received the mutiny medal, he having been actually engaged with the mutinous sepoys from Chittagong. In 1859, Mypak, a descendant of Gharib Newaz, made an attempt; he reached the valley, but was defeated under the western hills and fled. In 1862 he again invaded the valley ; his party was followed up by sepoys from Cachar, who had skirmishes with the raiders in the hills, but did not succeed in stopping them. Mypak succeeded in eluding the parties sent against him, including a guard of 50 men of the 44th Sikh Light Infantry under a European officer and attached to the Political Agency at that time, and got inside the Raja's enclosure at night. In the morning he and his party were easily overcome by the Manipuris, and Mypak wounded and taken prisoner.

The sepoys were not called upon to act. Mypak died in Manipur some two or three years afterwards. Several of his descendants and followers are still alive in the valley. Towards the end of 1864 or beginning of 1865, Kanai Sing made his second attempt, accompanied by about 200 followers. He only got as far as the Jiri river, where he was overtaken by a party of the 33rd Native Infantry and police, who completely defeated and dispersed the raiders, Kanai Sing making his escape.

In December 1866, the last of these raids took place, led by Gokul Sing, a younger son of Debendra Sing, who had not accompanied his father to Dacca. With about 100 followers he managed to reach the valley unmolested, though closely followed up by a party of sepoys and police from Cachar. The Manipuris sent out a party to meet him as soon as the news came in ; this party came up with the raiders under the hills to the west, about 10 miles from the capital. It being nearly dark when they came in contact, little was done, and the Raja's men proceeded to entrench themselves, proposing to attack the raiders in the morning. In the meantime, unknown to the Manipuris, the sepoys from Cachar were approaching their advance being observed by Gokul Sing, he and his adherents fled. The British force coming suddenly in the dark upon the force of entrenched Manipuris, and supposing them to be the enemy, at once attacked them. The Manipuris, on their side, were under the impression, the nighc being dark, that they in turn were being attacked by Gokul Sing and his men, defended themselves. An irregular firing on both sides was kept up all night, and in the morning the mistake was at once discoverd. In the meantime Gokul Sing and his adherents had got clear off. In this unfortunate affair several men were wounded on either side ; one man, a sepoy of the British force, afterwards died. Gokul Sing eluded pursuit until 1868, when he was apprehended by the police in Kuch Behar ; he was afterwards tried in Cachar and sentenced to seven years' imprisonment. The number of Manipuri princes now resident in the British provinces who are influential enough to make raids on Manipur are few. Debendra Sing died and his nephew, a son of Nar Sing, named Shaikar Sing, was detained at Dacca under British surveillance, as a politicel detenue, on an allowance of Rs. 20 a month. Kanai Sing, who had been at large since his last raid in 1865, was captured in 1871, and he, as well as Gokul Sing, are at Hazaribagh as exiles, and receive from the Manipur Durbar an allowance of Rs. 30 each per mensem. Kala *alias* Dayabant Sing, a grandson of Choorjet Sing, is also at Hazaribagh under

British surveillance. Nirjit Sing, another son of Debendra Sing, is living at Dacca with Shaikar Sing. Kanai Sing has an elder brother who resides in Agartolah in Tipperah, named Durjai Sing ; but there is nothing against him. Quirakpa, a grandson of Marjeet, formerly resided in the valley ; but as he wanted to raise disturbances, he was made to leave the country by the present Raja ; he now resides in Sylhet. Fourteen Manipuris, exiled from time to time for adhering to the cause of the raiders, have been released by Government at the request of the Maharaja. There seems to be no apprehension of any attempts to seize the raj from the Burmese side. Before the introduction of firearms at the time of the Burmese war, the numerous hill tribes now under control were then almost entirely independent, they being constantly at feud amongst themselves and with Manipur. The inhabitant of the valley had to meet the hillman with his own weapon, the spear, bow and arrow. Amongst the whole of the hill tribes at this period, the Tankuls and Luhupas were the most troublesome, occasionally making raids into the valley itself, but, like all hillmen afraid to quit the shelter of their hills for any distance, and easily beaten back by the pony cavalry of the State. Communication with the west at this time had scarcely any existence, and only large armed bodies of men could go with safety from Manipur valley towards Cachar. The Kaupuis and Marrings were then, as now, the most under control ; during the invasion of the Burmese, the hillmen on the line of the road invariably fled, and none of the Burmese operation involved the subjection of the hill tribes away from their lines of route. The whole of the hill tribes were unfriendly to the Burmese ; and although no organised attempt at resistence to their march was ever made by them, they lost no opportunity of annoying them and cutting off stragglers. After the defeat of the Burmese in Cachar, on their retreat they lost a number of men in the hills. As soon as the country became somewhat settled after the Burmese war, Raja Gambheer Sing turned his attention to the subjugation of the hill tribes. He, by the aid of the firearms now in his possession, speedily reduced the major portion of them to subjection. Before his death he reduced the Kaupuis completely, and brought the Taukuls, Luhupas, and Angami Nagas into fair order. During this period it was undoubtedly found necessary to resort occasionally to serve measures, and it may be supposed that the Manipuris, smarting under all that they had suffered from the hands of the tribes, made fatal use of their weapons ; but this excessive punishment has long ago ceased. During the time of Raja Gambheer Sing, two British officers, the late Captains Jenkins and Pemberton, accompanied by some 1,000 Manipuri sepoys, crossed the hills between the Manipur and Assam valleys; they met with much opposition from the warlike tribe of Angamis. Raids by any of the hill tribes have long ceased. Although it would not be profitable to detail every little raid or disturbance that has taken place of late years, some particulars with regard to raids by the Lushai tribe of Kukis may be found of interest. Until some 32 years ago, the tribes to the south in contact with the Manipuris were the Khongjai and Kom Kukis. On their being driven out by the Lushais, a series of raids and annoyances by the latter commenced, and continued until 1870-71. Disturbances have always been confined to the hills occupied by the Kaupai tribe of Nagas, although they once on their first appearance invaded the valley. This raid, the first by the Lushais, occurred about 32 years ago, when Raja Nar Sing occupied the gadi. The leader was Chief Vonolail, now dead. A village of Koogjais near the south of the valley was first destroyed, after which the Lushais entered the valley. The Manipuris in the villages adjacent turned out to the number of 500 with one mounted man armed with a spear to oppose them, and the Lushais were driven back with a loss of 10 men killed, the Manipuri loss being only 2. It is said that the one mounted man behaved with great bravery and inflicted great damage upon them ; after this raid, the only thing done was to establish a post at the point where they had entered the valley. About three years after the above occurrence, a village, named Nomidong or

Nungdang (the same village as was destroyed by the Lushais in October 1868, and in which they awaited the attack of the Manipuris sent against them), was cut up ; but it was never clearly ascertained whether the outrage was committed by Khongjais or Lushais. After an interval of about two years, during the incumbency of the Raja Chandra Kirti Sing, the thana of Kala Naga, containing only 10 men at the time, was suddenly attacked, the sepoys making good their escape. The Lushais numbered about 500, and the thana and surrounding villages were destroyed. The Lushais after this retreated, but returned in three months and committed great ravages in and around the Kala Naga range of hills, the few sepoys in the thana which had not been strengthened again retreating. Three hundred men were at once despatched from Manipur on this occession, but they arrived only to find that the Lushais had gone. The Kala Naga post was now strengthened, 300 men being posted in it. Shortly after this the Lushais returned for the third time and burnt a village close to the thana, evidently unaware of the reinforcement that had been thrown into the post. The Manipuris having concealed themselves, a party of them entered and the Manipuris, rushing from their concealment, captured ten of them before they could offer any resistance, the rest escaping. The prisoners were brought into Manipur, where they were detained for three or four years, after which nine of them succeeded in escaping from custody ; but they were all killed by Khongjai Kukis while trying to make their way back to their own country. After this, negotiations were opened with the Chief Vonolail. The surviving prisoner, who was a relative of his, was released on the Chief's giving a promise not to molest Manipur in the future. This promise the Lushais faithfully kept until 1868, when they again broke out and made raids on Mukti, Nungdang, etc, and attacked and burnt Kala Naga stockade. In 1872 the British Government sent an expeditionary force into the Lushai country, and punished the tribes that committed raids in the Cachar district. The Manipur Government, at the instance of the Government of India, also sent a force of

2,000 sepoys under two majors, with a view to co-operate with the Cachar column. They were detached at Chibu, in order to restrain Kamhow's tribe and guard the southern frontier. Though they were not employed in any active service, yet they succeeded in assisting and escorting some captives and refugees into their camp. On the return of the force in March 1872, some eight Lushai Chiefs, consisting of Dambum and others, came into Manipur and entered into a treaty with the Maharaja. The Government of India has also acknowledged the services rendered by the Manipur Dubar during the expedition, and presented the Raja with 500 Victoria muskets and 12 sporting rifles for himself and his princes. Three of his officers, Bolaram, Tangal, and Gokul, have also received khilluts from Government in recognition of their services.

Although the origin of British influence in the affairs of Manipur has been already referred to, it may be well here to give a connected account of its rise and the benefits it has conferred on the country. Up to the time of the first Burmese war, or rather shortly before it, little had been heard of the Manipuris. During the reign of Jaee Sing, Chingtung Khomba, negotiations were entered into with the British Government about 1762, with a view to obtain its assistance against the Burmese ; but nothing was effected. There is no knowledge among the Manipuris of the present day of any actual treaty, as mentioned in Aitchison's Treaties, page 121, having been concluded. In 1833, the treaty was concluded with Gambheer Sing. Of this treaty the Raja has no copy.

The present Manipur army had its origin in the old Manipur Levy, a body of 500 men raised by Raja Gambheer Sing in 1824, during the Burmese war. This body was armed and paid by the British Government and served under its directions. The original force of 500 was shortly increased to 1,000 and afterwards to 2,000, and two British officers were attached to it to superintend drill and discipline. These troops did good service in 1825. They cleared Manipur of the Burmese, and in the following year took the valley of Kubbo. In 1835 the one British officer which remained with the force was withdrawng, and since that date the efficiency of the Manipur troops has considerably deteriorated. The soldiers of Manipur receive no pay, but have land assigned to them according to rank, the value of a private sepoy's holding being about Rs. 7 per annum. Nominally, every man serves 10 days out of each 40; but were this rule strictly adhered to, the garrisoning of the more distant posts would be practically impossible. At such places, therefore, it is usual for the men to serve several months consecutively. Service may be said to be hereditary, the land with its obligations descending from father to son, so that the army increases with the population, and now numbers about 7,000, including 700 irregulars. The troops are supposed to be organised in regiments (battalions?). These are all infantry, except about 500 artillerymen, who have charge of eight old 3-pounder brass field guns, which are quite useless. The once celebrated Manipur cavalry, which performed brilliantly in the Burmese war, has practically disappeared, though a body of 400 still nominally exists. The reason for this extinction of the cavalry arm is that the breed of native ponies has very greatly deteriorated, while the import of ponies from Burma has been stopped since 1871 by the Burmese Government, without any apparent reason, so that to mount a force efficiently is now impossible. This is more unfortunate as Manipur was originally formidable principally on account of the number of mounted troops it could put into the field, and in a war with Burma the old pony cavalry would still be of immense service. According, however, to the Assam Trade Report of 1879-80, the Raja has stopped the export of ponies from his dominions, with the view of resuscitating the old breed. There is, therefore, some hope of the Manipur cavalry being in time re-established. The men of the infantry are of good physique, capable of bearing great fatigue, patient, willing, and obedient. They are always ready to march, carrying their own provisions, building their own huts, and, if necessary, entrenching themselves. Their independence, says Lieutenant-Colonel Johnstone, the Political Agent, is in striking contrast to the requirements of our own troops, who cannot move without a great number of coolies. The British officers who served with the Manipuris in the Burmese war thought well of their fighting qualities. If organised and again placed under British leaders, the Manipur troops would soon become a servicable body. Their own officers are very incompetent, and the present drill and training of the men is at the lowest ebb. About half the infantry is armed with smoothbore muskets. In addition to the regular State troops, some 700 Kuki irregulars are kept up. These act as scouts, etc., during expeditions. They are naturally more courageous and better soldiers than the Manipuris. Their arms are old muskets of various descriptions.

Excerpts from *Gazetteer of Manipur* by E.W. Dun.

APPENDIX-II

Religion of Manipuris

WOULD that it were possible to imitate or transcend the easy brevity of Father Sangermano, who declares that the people of Cassay worship the basil and other plants after the manner of the ancient Egyptians. Here we have the stately fabric of Hinduism with its elastic ease of accommodation, we have the fresh, healthy, indigenous system of animism, and as a result of the commingling of these forces at this point a medley of religious beliefs in which every phase of human imagination finds its place.

Hinduism is of comparatively recent origin, though the records of the Brahmin families in Manipur claim in some cases that the founder of the family settled in the valley at so remote a date as the middle of the Fifteenth century. To the royal will of Pamheiba, the monarch in whose reign the fortunes of the State reached their zenith, Hinduism owes its present position as the official religion of the State. At first the decrees of the king received but little obedience, and the opposition to the change centred mainly round the numerous members of the royal family who were supported, not unnaturally, by the *maibas*, the priests of the older religion. Religious dissent was treated with the same ruthless severity as was meted out to political opponents and wholesale banishments and execution drove the people into acceptance of the tenets of Hinduism. As a matter of fact the long reign of Chandra Kirti Singh witnessed the consolidation of Hinduism which had lost much of its hold on the people during the sad times of the Burmese occupation. Gambheer Sing once ordered a Brahmin who had failed to take due and proper charge of a pet goose which had been entrusted to his care, to eat the bird which had died from neglect, but in his son's time such an order was impossible.

The old order of things has not passed away by any means, and the *maiba*, the doctor and priest of the animistic system, still finds a livelihood despite the competition on the one hand of the Brahmin, and the Hospital Assistant on the other.

It is possible to discover at least four definite orders of spiritual beings who have crystallized out from the amorphous mass of animistic Deities. There are the *Lam Lai*, gods of the country-side who shade off into Nature Gods controlling the rain, the primal necessity of an agricultural community ; the *Umang Lai* or Deities of the Forest Jungle ; the *Imung Lai*, the Household Deities, Lords of the lives, the births and the deaths of individuals, and there are *Tribal Ancestors*, the ritual of whose worship is a strange compound of magic and Nature-worship. Beyond these Divine Beings, who possess in some sort a majesty of orderly decent behaviour, there are spirits of the mountain passes, spirits of the lakes and rivers, vampires and all the horrid legion of witchcraft. *Quot homines, tot daemones* with a surplusage of familiars who serve those fortunate few who are recognized as initiated into the mysteries.

It is not sound to regard these beliefs as "survivals" despite the official superstratum of Hinduism which exists in Manipur, solely in its exoteric form, without any of the subtle metaphysical doctrines which have been elaborated by the masters of esoteric Hinduism. The adherence of the people to the Vaishnavite doctrines which originated in Bengal, is maintained by the constant intercourse with the leaders of that community at Nadia. It is difficult to estimate the precise effect of Hinduism on the civilization of the people, for to the outward observer they seem to have adopted only the festivals, the outward ritual, the caste marks, and the exclusiveness of Hinduism, while all unmindful of its spirit and inward essentials. Colonel McCulloch remarked nearly fifty years ago that, "In fact their observances are only for appearance' sake, not the promptings of the heart," and his criticism seems as true now as when it was written. It is, perhaps, too early to predict the influence of British rule upon the religious ideas of the people. The Penal Code is in some aspects a code of morality resting in native view on superior force rather than on divine authority or intrinsic virtue. The inevitable rise in morality which ensues from security of life and property, from increasing wealth, and from a greater range of needs, is slowly becoming evident in Manipur, and must sooner or later exert an influence on the religious life of the country. The *maibas* frequently adapt their methods to the altered circumstances in which they now find themselves, and realize that the combination of croton oil and a charm is more efficacious than the charm alone. It is too much to expect them to give up the charm all at once.

In Manipur where Hinduism is a mark of respectability, it is never safe to rely on what men tell of their religion ; the only test is to ascertain what they do, and by this test we are justified in holding them to be still animists.

It is curious to note the complete absence of any traces of Buddhism in Manipur, although it is reasonably certain that in historic times there has been a steady flow of intercourse with Buddhistic Burma. The Shans under Samlongpha who invaded Manipur in the beginning of the Fifteenth century seem to have left no trace of their occupation of the State upon the religious belief of the people, for the records distinctly show that up to the formal introduction of Hinduism in the reign of Pamheiba the people buried their dead, ate meat, drank ardent spirits, and behaved just like the hill people of the present day. There is not a sign of contact with the lofty moral doctrines of Buddhism.

The chronicles enable us to know the names, and in some cases also the functions of a few of the popular Deities. Thus Panthoibi, to whose service Brahmins were appointed by Pamheiba (Gharib Newaz), is said to be the wife of Kbaba, probably the divine ancestor of the Khaba tribe, and to be the Deity of birth and death. She is certainly connected with the worship of the sun. The worship of Sena-Mehi by a prince was regarded as a sure preliminary to an attempt by the worshipper on the throne, and was reserved for the Raja alone. The Deity Lairema is associated with oneiromancy, and is also the name given to private Deities. Of her magical nature there can be no doubt, for the chronicles state that on the 17th *Langbon* (September), 1853, "There was a great fuss about Lairema Hooidompokpi. A sepoy reported to the Maharajah, that since Khuraijam established his God, Hooidompokpi, a considerable number of men died. The number of widowers and widows increased. The Maharajah ordered Losang Ningthou and Nongthonba to cause inquiry into this. It was turned out that there were two Lairemas." Of the Deity named Noongshaba we know that he is associated with a stone, and is probably, as his name would show (*ncng*= stone, and *shāba* = maker, i.e. maker of stones), the Deity of Creation of the rocks and stones. We do not know the reason why he, or Yumthai Lai, the Deity whom, on linguistic grounds, we may believe to be the establisher of houses, or the Deity Taibong Khombi, She who makes the earth to swell, should have been allowed to be served by Brahmins, while Pamheiba disestablished such Deities as Taibangkhaiba, He who divides the earth, or the clan Gods, or such Goddesses as Waihaiba. We know that Sena-mehi and Laima-ren are connected, and the name of the latter seems to mean "The Great Princess." We may conjecture that the female Deity Laishing-choubi was the wife of Laiching, the Deity whose abode is on the hill of that name. Of others, such as Wangpurel, Puthiba, Pukshore, Yumnam Lairema, Sarangthem Lamabi, Laisangthem Lamabi, we know little beyond the mere names. Some of them may be purely local, and their worship confined to the members of one family, or of one house, but even if *nomina* only, they are also *numina*, and rank above the vast crowd of *hing-chabis* or vampires (*hing* = alive, *cha* = to eat, that which eats live men), *lais hellois*, or demons, in which the people believe and fear being the basis of their ritual, which they try to propitiate. Colonel McCulloch states that there were three hundred such deities, and that they "are still propitiated by appropriate sacrifices of things abhorrent to real Hindoos."

Competent ethnologists declare that the conception of divine beings as "Gods" connotes, firstly, the relationship of members of a family, subject to one head, who may be Lord of all, or attenuated as merely *primus inter pares*; secondly, their representation in human form; thirdly, the association of moral benefit with their worship; fourthly, their presentation as idealized human beings; and fifthly, their occupation of a definite place in a definite cosmogonic system. Practically all these characteristics are lacking in Manipur. Indeed, it seems to be clear that deities like Panthoibi, Yumthai Lai, Laimaren, and Sena-mehi, are merely names of class spirits, for every householder is virtually the priest of these Deities just as in ancient Rome every household had its Vesta. There are images of deities hewn from stone, but the more powerful Deities, if we except Govindji, the God of the Royal family, are represented by rough stones, which Manipuris regard not exactly as the image of the Deity, but as his abode.

If the definition of ancestor-worship is strictly narrowed, we have in Manipur, among the Meithei only, the form of ancestor-worship which is practised by all Hindus, but if it be enlarged, as in the circumstances it ought to be, we find several curious phenomena to which attention should be given.

The worship of the clans which, seven in number, compose the Meithei nation or confederacy, clearly consists in the adoration and propitiation of the eponymous ancestors of the clan. The name of the tribal Deities is given as Luang pokpa, or ancestor of the Luangs, Khuman pokpa, ancestor of the Khumans, apparent exceptions to this being the tribal Deities of the Ningthaja and Angam clans, which are called Nongpok Ningthou, or the King of the East alias Pukhangba, whom we know from other sources to be the reputed ancestor of the clan in question (the Ningthaja), and Purairomba. The aliases of the other tribal Deities are Poiraiton, for the Luangs; Khamdingou, for the Khabananbas, Thangaren, for the Khumans, and Ngangningsing, for the Moirangs; and Nungaoyumthanagba, for the Chengleis.

The Hindu friends of the people have discovered for them a respectable genealogy by which they are descended from the Guru, the sage who is Lord of the Universe (*taibangpanbagi mapu*), but the accounts differ. In the version collected by me from the lips of a Manipuri, who had been a *sellungba*, or court officer, the Angoms spring from the brain of the sage, the Luangs from between his eyes, the Khabananbas from his ear, the Moirangs from his nostril, the Chenglei from his nose, the Kumul from his liver, and the Ningthaja from his spleen. The account prepared for me by a very respectable Bengali clerk states that the Ningthaja was born from his left eye, the Angom from his right eye, the Chenglei from his right ear, the Khabananba from his left ear, the Luang from his right nostril the Kumul from his left nostril, and the Moirang from his teeth. It is a delicate matter to assign a preference to one version rather than the other, but the symmetry of the second version is apt to excite the suspicion that the orthodoxy of the reporter may have misled him.

In the case of the ancestor of the Ningthaja clan, Pakhangba, we have the curious superstition that he still sometimes appears to men, but in the form of a snake, which reminds one of the Zulu belief that their ancestors assume the shapes of harmless brown snakes. Another instance which may help to explain the Pakhangba worship is afforded by the classical instance of the Romans, who held that the genius of every man resided in a serpent. Cicero (*De Divinatione*, i. 18, 36). tells how the death of the serpent, which was the genius of the Father of the Gracchi, presaged, and was soon followed by, the death of Tiberius. Recent investigations prove that the genius was the "external soul" so familiar in the folk tales of primitive peoples. Here the snake is the external soul of the Raja, the *piba* of the Ningthaja clan, and the head of the

Meitheis. Speaking of the religion of the people, Colonel McCulloch says that "The Raja's peculiar god is a species of snake called Pakung-ba, from which the Royal family claims descent. When it appears it is coaxed on to a cushion by the priestess in attendance, who then performs certain ceremonies to please it. This snake appears, they say, sometimes of great size, and when he does so it is indicative of his being displeased with something. But as long as he remains of diminutive form it is a sign that he is in good humour."

Whether connected immediately, or only remotely, with these associations of ancestor worship, I cannot say, but it is at least noteworthy that in the hymn which is addressed to the Raja by the man who is taking the sins of the country upon himself for the coming year, the Raja is addressed as "O Great God Pakhangba." This may of course, be merely an honorific phrase in harmony with the extravagant language used to the Raja, who on all occasions is addressed as if he were indeed a a Deity incarnate.

In contrasting the Meithei belief in Pakhangba with the Khasi faith in U Thlen, a clear account of which is given by Major Gurdon, the author of the monograph on the Khasis, several points of interest issue to notice at once. Pakhangba is an ancestral spirit worshipped by women, while among the matriarchal Khasis, where women are priests, U Thlen is not regarded apparently as an ancestor. Both are associated with the fortune of the family, but while U Thlen may move from one family to another, Pakhangba is associated only with the Raja directly, but indirectly with the whole State. Both vary in size, and it is noteworthy that the occasions when they assume their largest and most monstrous form, practically signify much the same thing, viz. portents of evil and misfortune. I have no evidence of human sacrifices to Pakhangba. In regard to the means adopted to get rid of the *thlen*, we may compare the transfer of sin by passing on the royal clothing with the sacrifice of property, money and ornaments which Khasis make when endeavouring to free themselves of the snake.

By the side of the road from Cachar not more than a mile from Bishenpur, are two small black stones which are reputed to be *Laiphams*, or places in which abides a "Lai," a being whose exact equivalency is difficult of determination. At Hiyangthang, about six miles distance from Imphal, is a temple of considerable fame, for here abides the Hindu Goddess Durga, who is known to have avenged an insult to her shrine by causing the death of the sacrilegious. In this temple is a rough black stone which naturally I was not allowed to see close at hand, but which, so far as I could distinguish it, was entirely unwrought. This was the *laipham* of the dreaded Goddess. One of the last civil cases that came to my notice was a dispute about an ammonite of inmense sanctity. In the course of the evidence it was proved that it had been looted from the Cachar Rajas at the beginning of the Nineteenth century, and passed into the possession of Gambheer Singh, upon whose death it came into the hands of his widow, mother of Chandra Kirti Singh, who took it with her, when, after the attempted assassination of Nur Singh, she fled to Sylhet. The stone was quite small, and its curious markings showed to all but the densest eyes that it was a thing of high sanctity. It brought good fortune to its possessor, and in the disturbances of 1891 was seized by Angao Sena, brother of the Raja, who was sent to the Andamans, and who gave it to a Brahmin who sold it to a Bengali, when it was rediscovered and claimed by the heirs of Sur Chandra, who alleged that as it had always been kept in the *bari* of the Royal Family, it was distinct from the regalia, and by the representatives of the present Raja, who asserted that it was impartible property attached to the office of Raja, while the Bengali claimed it for value had and received. I forget the finding of the learned Court on the case. In pre-Hindu times, as mentioned in the chronicles, the worship of stones—perhaps as *laipham*—was regularly practised, and the luck of the State was symbolized by the great Nongsha or animals of the Sun which, built of masonry to resemble stone, guarded the Kangla. In the chronicles we read that stones were looted from defeated Naga villages and brought down to Imphal. Now, at Maikel or Mekrimi, is a stone which, jealously guarded by the *khullakpa*, has great virtue in giving strength to warriors, and upon which no woman may look. I have heard it said in Manipur that it is worse by far to be reputed to be rich than to be rich, and the possession of so coveted an object as a war stone without doubt encouraged aggression and attack.

Lois worship Sena Mehi, and Laimaren the Imung Lai, and offer up pigs, dogs, ducks and fowls to them. The Sun God is worshipped by the people of Fayeng Loi in Sajibu (April), when they offer up a white fowl and a white pigeon. At Andro Loi offerings are made to both Sun and Moon, the latter being worshipped every month on an auspicious day in the last quarter of the moon. They offer up each year a pig in honour of the Umang Lai or Deities, who control the prosperity of the crops, as rain and weather Gods. Panam Ningthou and Purairomba are their Umang Lai, while Khabru is the Umang Lai of Fayeng, and of Sengmai, where they told me he was the Lam Lai or God of the countryside. They also worship the clan God, whose names coincide with those of the clan Gods of certain Meithei clans. Fayeng Lois assert that their ancestors were Meng-khong-ba and Hameng-mitpa.

Colone McCulloch states that "The Dussera, or as it is called in Munipore *Kwaktalba*, is the principal festival introduced with Hinduism. At it the tributaries lay presents before the Raja and renew their engagements of submission. Honorary dresses, plumes of feathers, and other baubles which are highly prized, are distributed to persons who, during the past year, may have distinguished themselves, or to others who, at some former period, had done so, but whose merit had passed unrewarded." *Kwaktalba* seems to mean the chasing of the crow (from *kwak*=a crow, and *talba*=to chase or pursue).

The Holi attracts a gay crowd of women to the capital who are seldom slow to take due advantage of the licence permitted to them, but from the coincidence of so many animistic or other festivals with those of Hinduism, a phenomenon which admits of an easy explanation, it is perhaps wiser to say that attention is paid to all and each of the various festivals which are observed by the devout among Hindus of the Vaishnavite order.

The great and general religious festival of the *Laiharaoba*, or the rejoicing of the Gods (*Lai*=Deity, and *haraoba*=to be merry or to make merry), is thus described by Colonel McCulloch, "Particular families have particular gods, and these at stated periods they worship, or literally 'make happy'. This worship consists in a number of married women and unmarried girls, led by priestesses, accompanied by a party of men and boys all in dresses of a former time, dancing and singing, and performing various evolutions in the holy presence. The women carry in their hands fruits, etc., part of which is presented to the deity, and part scrambled for by the girls. In some instances the god is represented by an image, but often there is no such representation, and a place is merely prepared in which he is supposed to be during the worship. The presence of the god, however, in either way, impresses the worshippers with no awe; on the contrary, it appears to be a cause of fun and jollity."

The next great festival to which attention is now to be drawn is the *Chirouba*, a name which my informant, a Hindu of high caste from Bengal, stated to be connected with *charak puja*, a derivation with which it is impossible to agree. The festival is closely connected with the choice of a *chahitaba* or name-giver for the coming year, and takes place at the end of the Manipuri month, Lamda, which corresponds with the middle of April. The Deity in whose particular honour the festival is held, is Senamehi, the administrator, as my friend and informant says, of the Universe. It is regarded as an auspicious day, and on it no work is done except that they clean their houses out very carefully. They wear new clothes and break all their old *Chaphus* or earthenware cooking pots and eat alone without any guests. It is a day of powerful influence on the coming year, and on it takes place the selection of the *chahitaba*, the man who gives his name to the year, who bears all the sins of the people for the year, and whose luck, good or ill, influences the luck of the whole country. The derivation of the word *chahitaba* is obscure. *Kum*, the word for a year in so many Tibeto-Burman dialects, is not unknown in Meithei, but *chahi* is peculiar to it. Some say that it is connected with the word *chahi* or *chai*=a stick, and *taba*, means to count, to count by sticks, the practice of the Manipuris being to calculate by means of a heap of sticks. Others derive it from *chahi*=a year, and *taba*=to fall, because the fall of one year implies the commencement of a new year. According to another opinion, *chahi* bears the meaning of a year, and *taba* is connected with the root *takpa*=to show or indicate to point out—thus making the phrase to mean the person who indicates or names the year.

All reckonings of time are made by *chahitibas* as well as by the Hindu system, and there are still men in the State who can repeat all the *chahitabas* from the institution of the custom by Kiamba, in about 1485, who appointed Hiang Loi Namoi Chaoba to be the first *chahitaba*.

The *maibas* nominate the man and compare his horoscope with those of the Raja and the State generally, and if they satisfactorily correspond, as is natural they should, the candidate together with the outgoing *chahitaba*, appears before the Raja and the assembled multitudes when, after worshipping his spiritual director, the Guru and his own God (probably his tribal deity), the retiring *chahitaba* then addresses the incoming officer in the following terms: "My friend, I bore and took away all evil spirits and sins from the Raja and his people during the last year. Do thou likewise from to-morrow until the next Chirouba." Then the incoming *chahitaba* thus addresses the Raja : "O son of heaven, Ruler of the Kings, great and ancient Lord, Incarnation of God, the great Lord Pakhangba, Master of the bright Sun, Lord of the Plain and Despot of the Hills, whose kingdom is from the hills on the east to the mountains on the west, the old year perishes, the new cometh. New is the sun of the new year, and bright as the new sun shalt thou be, and mild withal as the moon. May thy beauty and thy strength grow with the growth of the new year. From to-day I will bear on my head all thy sins, diseases, misfortunes, shame, mischief, all that is aimed in battle against thee, all that threatens thee, all that is bad and hurtful for thee and thy kingdom." The Raja then gives the new *chahitaba* a number of gifts, including a basket of salt. The *chahitaba* is exempt from *lalup*, and receives many privileges from the State. The *chahitaba* offers brass plates accompanied by sacred offerings of fruit and flowers to the Raja, to the *maiba* and attendants of the Deity Pakhangba, to the *maiba loisang* or College of the *Maibas*, (exorcists' office as the term is translated by my Hindu friend) to the College of the Astrologers, to the Maharani, to the Overseer of the Royal stores, and last, not least, to the Hindu Deity Govindji, the Family God of the Royal family.

It is interesting to note that certain classes of persons are ineligible for this important office, such as Rajkumars, possibly because they are never out of the line of succession and therefore undesirable, Panggans or Manipuri Musalmans, Nagas who find consolation in an ampler dietory, and Thangjams and Konsams, blacksmiths and brassworkers. I can give no reason for the ineligibility of the two last classes, except that it is possible that they occupy or once occupied so low a position in society that they were excluded.

The appointment of a *chahitaba* rests on the desire to find a scapegoat to bear the sins of the community or of the individual Raja, the idea which is clearly the motive of the scapegoat ceremony which takes place at the foot of the holy hill Khabru on the grassy plain, to which the significant name Kaithenmanbi, the meeting place of the ghosts, has been given (*Kaithen*=market or gathering place, *manbi* from *manba*=to resemble, to appear). Thither annually the Raja went in solemn procession to sacrifice a white goat, male without blemish, to the God Khabru whose abode it was, and to leave there fish and an offering of new clothes. But there come times when such ordinary devices as these fail of their purpose, and it is necessary to have recourse to special sin-takers. Generally some criminal is found to take upon himself the guilt of the Raja and Rani who, clad in fine robes, ascend a staging erected in the bazar beneath which crouches the sin-taker. The Raja and Rani then bathe in the screened tent on the stage, and the water they use in their ablutions, drops over the man below, to whom they give their robes and sins. Clad in new raiment, the Raja and his consort mix among their people until evening of that day, when they retire into a seclusion which may last for a week, and during which they are said to be *namungba*, sacred or *tabu*.

Sometimes the transference of sins has been satisfactorily accomplished by the simple device of presenting the Royal cloth to a "sin-taker."

More than one ethnologist of note has pointed out that among communities which are animistic and which subsist by agriculture, rain-worship assumes peculiar importance, and to this statement the state of things in Manipur is no exception. There are Hindu ceremonies, performed by Brahmins, such as the milking of 108 milch cows before the temple of Govindji, or the presence of the images of Radha Krishna at the river bank, when the people cry aloud for rain and the priests mutter *mantras*. But the great characteristic of the rites of the pre-Hindu system is the management of these rites by the *maiba*, the *piba*, or in more important cases by the Raja, who is, in fact, regarded not only as a living Deity, but as the head of the old State religion and the secular head of the whole people, including the Ningthaja or Royal clan. The hill which rises to the east of Imphal, and which is called Nongmaiching, is the scene of a rain-compelling ceremony. On the upper slopes there is a stone which bears a fanciful resemblance to an umbrella, and the Raja used to climb thither in state to take water from a deep spring below and pour it over this stone, obviously a case of imitative magic. It was said that to erect an iron umbrella on the hill was an almost sure method of getting rain, when occasion needed. And there are many other rites and ceremonies all of which are destined to provide the thirsty land with the rain, without which all are about to die, and at all of which the Raja should be present.

Sometimes his great racing-boat was dragged through the mud and slime of the empty moat with the Raja and his semi-sacred father-in-law, the Angom Ningthou, seated together in the stern.

The Kangla, the place where the most mysterious rites pertaining to the coronation of the Raja were performed, was the scene of a ceremony of which I have never been able to get a proper or intelligible account. Suffice to say that whatever happened there, it was sufficient to give rise to the story that human sacrifices had been made in the dire extremity of the country, for in older times, as I was told, the blood of some captive would have brought the rain. The sacrifice of ponies for this purpose may be due to the operation of what has been called the law of substitution. But the activity of the people does not confine itself to merely witnessing these official exhibitions. The men, headed on the worst occasions of prolonged drought by the Raja, strip themselves of all their clothes and stand in the broad ways of Imphal cursing one another to the fullest extent of an expressive language. The women at night gather in a field outside the town, strip themselves and throw their *dhan* pounders into a neighbouring pool in the river and make their way home by byways. Of course there is the legend of a Peeping Tom, for whose outrage on the royal decency the country went rainless for a whole year. To some *maiba* the wicked act was revealed in a dream, and then justice was done and the country saved.

The Kumul Ningthou worships the Tribal Deity Okparen on behalf of the clan whenever rain is needed. He has to abstain from meat of any kind and from all sexual intercourse before this *puja*. To purify him water is poured over his head by a virgin from a new jar which is promptly broken. He does not worship Sena Mehi or Laimaren.

Dr. Brown states that "in the event of Munniporie Hindu losing his caste from any reasons, the individual has to take, up his abode in a Naga village, eating with the inhabitants.

Its object seems to be to start the offender afresh from the lowest class." This is denied by many but has all the natural appearance of a purificatory rite. Does this throw any real light on the "affinities" of the Meitheis ?

Each clan has its tribal Deity, and certain flowers, fruits, etc., are set aside for each Deity. Thus the Ningthaja clan offer the lotus, the lime, the mahasir fish, the *mongba*—a small rat, I believe. Their special day is Monday (Ningthoukaba), and their special month is Inga.

Side by side with the Brahmin, there exist the priests and priestesses of the animistic faith who are called *maibas* and *maibis*, a word which also connotes, nowadays, the practice of the healing art because, as the language of the people clearly tells, a man is said to be ill (*a-na-ba*) when he is possessed by a *nat*. The heads of the clans are priests, and assume charge of the ritual of the tribal worship, while the Raja, the head of the Ningthaja clan and the head of the whole confederacy, is the high priest of the country.

The chronicles of the State contain frequent and early mention of the *maibas*, while we have it on the authority of Colonel McCulloch that the *maibis* "owe their institution to a princess who flourished hundreds of years ago, but whether they have preserved all their original characteristics I cannot certainly affirm. At present any woman who pretends to have had a 'call' from the deity or demon, may become a priestess. That she has had such call is evidenced by incoherent language and tremblings, as if possessed by the demon. After passing her novitiate she becomes one of the body and practises with the rest on the credulity of the people. They put some rice or some of the coins of the country into a basket, and turning it about with incantations, they pretend to divine from it. They dress in white." Elsewhere he remarks that the priestess looks after Pakhangba, the snake.

The *maiba* is for the most part a medical practitioner with a good deal of empiric knowledge, which he supplements with brazen ingenuity, but he is also the rain doctor to whom men turn for help after the failure of all other methods. He is employed in all cases where purely magical ceremonies are performed, a sure sign of his true position.

The *pibas* or heads of the clans are now dignified officers holding in the case of the *pibas* of the Angom, Kumul and Luang clans, the title of Ningthou or king. They officiate at the annual ceremonies, which seem to be in honour of the eponymous tribal ancestor, or which are connected with the crops, and special precautions have to be taken against any impurity on their part. But pre-eminent above them all is the Meithei Ningthou, who is not only the head or *piba* of the Ningthaja clan, but the chief of his people as well. His appearances in a priestly capacity are infrequent, and limited to some great calamity, such as prolonged drought, when he will intercede with the powers that be, on behalf of his pepole. It is needless to say that the sacred person of the Raja is protected by many *tabus*. Some pertain to his royal office, while others are as distinctly intended to guard his priestly sanctity from pollution. He may in times of special distress avert the wrath of heaven by transferring his sins and those of the principal Rani to some wretched criminal, who thereby obtains a partial remission of his sentence and as a reward receives the discarded robes of the royal pair. In this connection it may be mentioned that the *chahitaba*, the man who gives his name to the year, and who for the space of one year takes upon himself the sins of the whole people, enjoys for the term of his office a sanctity which is indistinguishable from that of the priest. Full details of the method and rites of appointing the *chahitaba* have been given above.

Indra, the Sky God, has his counterpart in the Meithei system, where the Deity Sorarel possesses all the attributes generally assigned to Indra, with whom he is now identified by the ingenious Hindus. The lofty hills which surround the valley are named after the Deities whose abode they are held to be. Khabru, on the north-west, looks down on the plain of Kaithenmanbi, the meeting-place of the spirits, and thither annually, in olden times, the Raja used to go in state to propitiate the Deity. When the thunder bursts on the summit of the mountain, men say the God fires his cannon ; when they see in winter the snow fall on the topmost peak, the God is spreading his cloth. There are Thangjing, Marjing, Laiching, and the sacred hill, Nongmaiching, which seems to be derived from *Nong* = sun or rain, *mai* = face or in front of, and *ching* hill, and to mean the hill that fronts the rain ar sun. Does the Deity give the name to the hill, not the hill the name to the Deity ?

From the ballad of Numit kappa we know that they believed that once upon a time there were two Sun Gods riding on white horses, and now the moon is the faint pale image of the one that was wounded. Beneath the earth lives the earthquake Deity who shakes the earth, and to whom they pray *nga chak*, "Spare us our fish and rice," whenever he shakes the earth.

There are many rain *pujas*, but there does not seem to be any one rain Deity. In some cases the prayers of the worshippers are addressed to the tribal ancestor, and the *puja* performed entirely by the *piba* or head of the tribe. If we have not a thunder Deity, we have at least the legend of a Thunder Deity enshrined in the language of the people. In Meithei the word for lightning is *nong-thang-kup-pa,* which is derived from *nong* = rain, *thang* = *dao, kup* = to flash, and has therefore the meaning of the flash of the *doa* of the Rain God. Now among the Thados we find the legend of the Rain Deity a mighty hunter coming home aweary from the chase and thirsty. Wroth was he when he found that his wife had no *zu* ready for him, and he brandished his *dao* at her, roaring hoarse threats of punishment for her neglect of her wifely duties, and in his haste to quench his mighty thirst, he spilt the drink. It is curious to observe the *lacuna* ; the Thados have the tale but not the word, while the Meitheis have the word but not the tale.

The Meitheis follow the ordinary rules of modern Vaishnavites in the matter of birth ceremonies, but have, in addition, a small *puja* in honour of the Imung Lai or the Household God, which is performed by the head of the household. This latter ceremony is, of course, non-Hindu.

Both Colonel McCulloch and Dr. Brown give explanations of the system of naming employed by the Meitheis, and concur in regarding the names as in many cases derived either from the profession or some personal peculiarity of the founder of the family. Colonel McCulloch says that "individuals are spoken of and known by their surnames ; the *laiming*, or if I may use the expression, the Christian name, being seldom known to or used by any but the nearest relatives. All but the Royal family have surnames. The Christian name is written last. The introduction of surnames took place in the reign of Chalamba, about two hundred years ago, and *laiming* since the profession of Hindooism. The surnames are evidently derived from some peculiarity in the individuals who first bore them. The oldest family of Brahmins in the country is called Hungoibum. *Hungoi* means a frog, and that such a name should be given to a person who bathed so much frequently than Munniporees had been accustomed to see, seems very natural. The same is the case with almost every family ; all the surnames indicating either the profession or some peculiarity of its original holder."

Dr. Brown treats the matter in a different manner, and says that "The names of the Munnipories are given on rather a complicated system, which may now be explained. In the first place, all the inhabitants have what is called a *yoom-nak*, or family name, corresponding with our surnames ; some of these names are evidently derived from the ancestor's employment, as *Lairik-yem-bum* corresponding with our English name, 'Clerk or Scrivener' *Phoorit-sa-bum*, tailor ; *Thangjaba*, smith, etc., etc. Next is the Hindoo name given by the astrologers, according to Hindoo custom, and, lastly, a nickname, or pet name, given to them when children, and by which they are known all their lives frequently. Sometimes the family name is alone used, occasionally the Hindoo, and very often the nickname ; it is thus no easy matter some times to identify a Munniporie by name. I give a few examples of complete names, with their meanings when known.

Family name . . Lairik-yem-bum (writer).
Hindoo name . . Guneshur.
Pet name . . . Baboo or Bapoo.

Family name . . Phoorit-sa-bum (tailor).
Hindoo name . . Moonee Ram.
Pet name or nickname . Tuba Lokpa.

It thus appears that there is a name which is not permitted to be common property, that there is generally a nickname, or pet name, which is known to and used by the world at large, and that the family, or *yumnak* name, is derived from either the occupation or some peculiarity of the original founder of the family—that is to say, the *yumnak* name is in origin descriptive in much the same way as the nickname or supplementary name now is.

Furthermore, it should be mentioned that it is customary for the Raja to assume a formal name on or after his accession by which he is described in all official documeuts. Thus, the Maharaja Chandra Kiriti Singh was also known as Nowchingleng Nongdren Khomba after the year 1870, though he actually succeeded to the throne many years before that date. Thus the Raja, to whose reforming zeal the country owes the introduction of Hinduism, is variously known as Gharib Newaz, Pamheiba, or Moianba. Doubtless the explanation of some, at least, of the Royal names is that they commemorate some incident or exploit which occurred during the reign, such as that of Khagenba, whose name may possibly mean "Conqueror of the Chinese" (from *Khagi* = Chinese, and *yanba* = to slaughter, or defeat).

The assumption of the sacred thread by a Meithei is regarded as proper when a lad has reached man's estate, but it is often delayed, and may be postponed without serious inconvenience. There is a curious custom which requires the eldest son of the Raja, when twelve years of age, to go into the jungles alone as a sign that he possesses the necessary strength and courage, and cut twelve bundles of fire-wood with a silver-hilted *dao*, which, tradition says, was presented to Khagenba by the King of Pong, that mysterious kingdom whose exact geographical position has vexed the minds of so many inquirers, who either forgot, or were never acquainted with, the peculiar laxity of the Meitheis in regard to the geography of unknown countries. The people of Pong were the Shans beyond their ken who visited them, and it is quite legitimate to conclude that the kingdom of Pong meant the powers who at the time were in supreme authority in the Shan States with which the Meitheis had dealings.

The following excellent note by Mr. H.A. Colquhoun, I.C.S., gives all that can be desired in the way of an account of the marriage rites in vogue among the Meitheis :—"The usual marriage ceremony is that known as Prajapati or Brahma. After the parents have settled the preliminaries, the announcement of the forthcoming marriage or *Yathang thaba* takes place. This is followed by offerings of sweetmeats or *heijapot* on three separate occasions from the bridegroom to the bride's family. The actual ceremony is held at the bride's house; a large party assembles, and a *Kirtan* is held, the bride sitting in front of the bridegroom. Mantras are recited, and the ancestry of the pair up to the great-grand-parents is repeated. The *sapta pradakhsin* follows : the bride walking ceremonially seven times around the groom and casting flowers upon him; garlands (*leipareng*) are placed on both, and the company prostrate themselves before them. They are then seated side by side, and their *innaphi*, or *chadars*, are fastened together. The *Hari Kirtan*, and the prostration are again repeated. The bride then enters the cooking-room followed by the groom. The pair sit on the same mat, and place *pan* (*panna khutap*), and subsequently sweetmeats (*kangsubi*) in each other's mouths. Offerings of *pan* are made to them by friends and relatives. The party then marches to the bridegroom's house, the bride being carried in a litter at the head of the party. A large and substantial wooden bed is a prominent feature of the procession. On the sixth day following there is a feast at the house of the bride's family, and the ceremony is then complete.

"Other forms of marriage are also practised, the Sampati Rajbibaha, Rakshasa and Gandharva, the latter being, of course, constituted by simple cohabitation."

Colonel McCulloch states that "Although to become man and wife it is not necessary that the marriage ceremony should be performed, still it is usually performed, but as often after as before cohabitation." It should be noted that the penalty on irregular marriages is the loss of the right to obtain offices about the Royal person and the inquiries which were necessitated by the census of 1901 caused some genuine alarm from the rumours sedulously spread that as in the days of that stern old despot Chandra Kirti Singh, severe punishments awaited those who had taken advantage of the laxity of the British administration in these matters to contract connubial alliances without the usual sanction of the Brahmin. The fact is that most Manipuris regard cohabitation and public acknowledgment as sufficient, provided that due regard has been paid to the rules restricting marriage to members of the Meithei tribes and forbidding the intermarriage of persons of the same clan, *salei*.

Among the Lois gifts are exchanged and a feast prepared which culminates in the sacrifice to the Imung Lai, to the Lam Lai, and to the Umang Lai.

At Sengmai, where the manufacture of ardent spirits is the chief industry, presents of *zu* were offered to the girl's parents when the marriage was under discussion. If these gifts were peremptorily refused nothing further happened, but if the first invitation was accepted, the matter came into the range of practical politics and omens were taken to ascertain whether or not the marriage was favourably regarded by divine authority. Eventually the day was fixed, and the bride-price handed over, and the feast made ready.

All the rites and ceremonies consequent on the death of a Meithei are in the hands of the Brahmins, and there is therefore no feature to which attention should be specially drawn.

Sepulture is only allowed in the case of children dying under the age of two years, and the burial takes place by preference on the bank of some river. I agree with Mr. Colquhoun in regarding the use of a box-like structure on the funeral pyres as a trace of the former method of sepulture for adults. It is well known that up to the advent of Hinduism, the dead were buried, and the chronicles mention the enactment by Khagenba of a rule that the dead were to be buried outside the enclosures of the houses. Gharib Newaz ordered the Manipuris to exhume the bodies of their ancestors, which they formerly used to bury inside their compounds. At a later date in his reign, in the year 1724, Gharib Newaz exhumed the bones of his ancestors and cremated them on the banks of the Engthe River, and from that time ordered his subjects to burn their dead. The system of cremation in vogue among the Meitheis is very thorough, as Mr. Colquhoun remarks, and the frontal bone is preserved and thrown in the Ganges at a later date, as opportunity arises.

The corpse is never carried over the threshold of the main door, sometimes a hole is cut in a wall or the tiny side entrance used.

Mention has been made of the various Hindu festivals such as the *Dussera*, and of the festival which is tribal in reality known as the *Laiharaoba*. It is doubtful whether the *waritabas* or parties given by wealthy folk, at which *iseisakpas*, or wandring minstrels, recite the stories of the wanderings of Ching thangkhomba, or of the unhappy loves of Khamba and Thoibi or the adventures of Numit kappa, are of a religious nature, but so closely are the threads of religion interwoven in the web of life of the people, that strange as it may seem to those who are accustomed to a religious system which provides for one day of the week only, it is probably just to mention these gatherings in this place. Recited in a dialect which is unintelligible to the listeners, despite the nasality of the tone in which they are recited, and despite the jangling accompaniment of the *pena*, these ballads possess something of real beauty. The audience knows not the exact import of the words they hear, but it knows the sad, the mirthful passages as they occur, and greets them with tears or with appropriate laughter. Meitheis or Moirangs, they listen with avidity to the trials of Khamba and Thoibi, the ballad which cannot fail to remind one of the stories of the Trials of Hercules, and which is held true by all, for to this day are not the clothes worn by these worthies still preserved in the temple at Moirang ?

The detrition of the ancient customs which began by the introduction of Hinduism, has moved on with increasing rapidity since the country became the prey of the Burmese forces under Aloung Pra and his successors, prevents us from estimating the real extent to which the *genna* customs used to prevail among the Manipuris. If to-day they have not the thing itself, they have at least the memory of it in the word *namungba*, which covers precisely the same range of ideas as the word *genna*. There are even survivals of practices which among Nagas we call *genna*, and these I will now proceed to discuss.

It will be seen that among Naga tribes the head of the clan is divided from the common herd by *gennas* of food and speech. Thus it is *namungba* for any Manipuri to address the Raja except in a peculiar vocabulary. We may compare this with the prohibition against the use of certain profane words by priests and kings. Again they say that food cooked in a pot which has been used before, is *namungba* to the Raja. Indeed, of every prohibition which rests on vague indefinable sanctions, they use the term *namungba*. Each clan in Manipur regards some object as *namungba* to it, and believes that if by inadvertence some member of the clan touches one of these objects he will die a mysterious death, or suffer from some incurable, incomprehensible disease, pine away and die. The object which is *tabu* to the Ningthaja clan is a reed, that to the Moirangs the buffalo, in the case of the Kumuls it is a fish. Again, if a man falls from a tree, the elders of his clan may gather round that tree and solemnly declare it, even all others of its kind, to be *namungba* to their tribesmen. Yet another instance of the working of ideas which in other parts of the world have elaborated the system of *tabu.* the trees which crown the tumulus in Imphal, beneath which, according to common tradition, repose the bones of the Moirangs who fell in the last great battle with the Meitheis, are *namungba* to the men of Moirang to this day, and between them no Moirang may go, for, if one were so bold as to venture through, ruin would overwhelm his fellow clansmen.

It is remarkable that to this day the Moirangs whom I have described as still clinging to their independence and separateness, preserve something like a system of *genna,* participated in by the whole clan, and, like the Naga *gennas*, held periodically and connected with the times and seasons of cultivation.

Beyond these few cases it is now impossible to describe the *genna* system as it once existed ; but I hope I have said enough to show that to this present day the fundamental ideas which underlie all *genna* rituals, are alive and active in Manipur.

To the curious in such matters the relationship of the three roots, *mang* = dream, *mung* [*namungba* = *la* = *id* = *lai*= Deity + *mung*] and *mung* = to be polluted or to be destroyed, may be commended for further investigation. We know that the legends of the country declare that the Gods appeared in dreams and gave orders as to all sorts of affairs, thus legislating through the mouth of the dreamers. *Mang-ba* (to be polluted) has a religious significance, for it applies to cases of ceremonial pollution. If we admitted, and it is temptingly easy to do so, that *namungba* is derived from *La* = God and *mung* (? =*mang* or ? =*mang*), we should have an interesting instance of philology assisting our theory gratuitously. We have high authority for connecting the Meithei word *ising* with the Tibetan *chhu,* so that perhaps these humble guesses at philological truth are not of the order which neglects the consonants and is rude to the vowels. In fact, the connection between divine appearances in dreams, sacred prohibitions, *tabu* and pollution, is of the closest.

Excerpts from *The Meitheis* by T.C. Hodson